To Enter Aquarius

The symbol on the front cover is a universal symbol depicting the five elements, i.e., fire, water, earth, air and ether. Borrowed from Dr Murdo McDonald Bayne's book, *The Higher Powers You Can Use* (p. 75).

Donald G. Wilson Phd., Ms.

TO ENTER AQUARIUS

The Oracle Press

Published by The Oracle Press
P.O. Box 121 Montville Qld 4560 Australia

National Library of Australia

ISBN 1 876308 16 8

Printed by Watson and Ferguson & Co., Moorooka, Qld. 4105

Contents

Acknowledgements

Sometimes there comes an event in our lives that serves as a turning point.

These events can come in many different forms; some of sorrow, some of elation, some of surprise or it may be such a simple act of having a book placed in your hand.

I was never one for reading. I could probably count on one hand the number of books that I had read by the age of 19. Such was my experience when more than 30 years ago my father-in-law, John Nelson Power, gave me a book entitled, *Divine Healing of Mind and Body*, by Dr Murdo MacDonald-Bayne.

I was working in the Copper Mines at Mt Isa in northwest Queensland Australia at the time. I lived in the mine's barracks, which in those days was quite rough and the last place one would expect to experience a spiritual awakening.

Yet amidst the noise and ruckus, as I turned page after page of this magic book, I found myself floating around the room in absolute awe, hungrily digesting every word as if I had not truly eaten in a long time.

In the following years I sought every book that Dr Murdo MacDonald-Bayne (affectionately referred to as Dr Mac) had written and I had some incredulous experiences that served to encourage me to continue my studies.

Unfortunately, these writings are now long out of print so I wrote this book to share with the reader some of Dr Mac's teachings along with other learning that has assisted me on the path.

Foreword

This book is written for the benefit of the earnest seeker. For those of you who have the courage to step out and dare to walk the path of individuality and enlightenment.

I draw your attention to the fact that by way of universal law, once you have been given the enclosed information regardless whether you accept it or not, you will be automatically more responsible and accountable for your life. For example, your actions, motives, thoughts, words and deeds – one to another.

We are all walking this path, mostly unconsciously and ignorant of the forces at play around us and the assistance of those who serve us from beyond the flesh. But for those of you who are at the stage where you deliberately seek to set out on this path of truth and light, then let your faith light the way and let your courage be your staff.

The key is to look within. The world external to the self is in reality an illusion. To look within indeed requires the courage of the unflinching warrior for you soon come to learn that we ourselves are our own greatest enemy.

These writings are designed so that the earnest seeker may be equipped with informed information and put into practice certain simple exercises that leads the neophyte from confusion to enlightenment.

Introduction

The arrival of the new millennium is causing great excitement, plans and anticipation.

As the hour of midnight December 31st 1999 tracks westward across the globe; no doubt celebrations will be ignited in every country on Earth, each reflecting their own unique traditional way to welcome in the new age.

Astrological new ages, unlike new years, do not start at one minute past midnight, December 31st. These ages are a gradual merging over hundreds of years with the old outgoing age slowly and reluctantly giving way to what are at first subtle or non-intrusive influences. With the passing of time these influences gradually seep into every area of celestial and terrestrial expression. The influence penetrates the mind and emotions, remoulding our attitudes and outlook in our laws, religions and social structure and prompting new discoveries in science.

The Age of Aquarius is being heralded as a Golden Age. For this reason it is with great expectations that this new era will usher in a time of peace and harmony throughout the Earth. Its key words are Unity and Brotherhood.

While it is true that new astrological ages manifest themselves despite the actions or non-actions of man, it is also true that our actions or non-actions can decide if the transition will be smooth or eventful.

We need to realise, however, that these times bring with them opportunities for mankind both individually and collectively to take a giant leap forward along the path of truth and light. This particular transition from

Pisces to Aquarius is a transition from one extreme to another – from a state of spiritual ignorance to a state of enlightenment.

At the beginning of the Age of Pisces the Master Jesus showed mankind by virtue of demonstration the way to enlightenment. These teachings, although carried on by the few over the past two thousand years, were quickly smothered by man's concepts of the teachings and it came to be that the concepts rather than the true teachings themselves were fed to the multitudes.

The situation we find ourselves in today is spiritual poverty. All over the world there is unrest, insecurity and a sense of divine discontent touches everyone. Mankind has spread and populated almost every corner of the globe bringing with him his insatiable thirst for material wealth and comfort, which in turn has resulted in the rape and violation of the Earth itself.

The Age of Aquarius will manifest on Earth and as its influence builds and we approach the great crescendo, man will be forced by way of necessity to turn from his obsession of the material plane and realise the ONENESS of all life.

At this time now there is an interplay of spiritual forces on the Earth to offset the ignorance of man. This gives an opportunity for those who are sincere in heart to take advantage of this time and by virtue of applying the Christ principles, rise above the confusion, frustration and fear and take on the mantle of the Christ Self.

To walk the path does not require a great wealth of knowledge. The process is more of letting go, freeing the mind of concepts and misconceptions, thus allowing the spiritual self that you really are to manifest in your life and circumstances. What is required is that the aspirant be sincere in his quest and work towards purity of heart. For indeed it is the heart that is the doorway, the eye and the ear of the spirit.

The following writings are designed firstly to put forward an alternative view of the plan of creation and the part that man plays during his evolutionary journey. Secondly, to give practical information that, if put into practice, will assist those who set out on the path in earnest with the courage, thus inspiring others by virtue of their way of life.

For truth cannot be spoken, it can only be lived. Truth is a way of life. A way of life that is demonstrated not by the intellect, nor indeed by phenomena but only by a heart that is quick in its application of love and a mind that is the humble.

Chapter One

The infinite manifested

In Genesis 1-26 we read, "Let 'us' make man in our 'image' and likeness." It is important to know who is the 'us'. If God is all there is, as I will explain, then who is this 'us' that Genesis is referring to?

The 'us' is referring to the Trinity. The Trinity from a metaphysical point of view is 'divine consciousness', 'divine intelligence' and 'divine substance', which are the three facets of the one.

When we are familiar with universal law we find that divine consciousness, which is the male or positive aspect 'directs'. In other words it is where the plan or desire first originates.

Divine intelligence is the female or negative aspect and it 'out-pictures' that which is in the consciousness. It takes the blueprint of the plan or desire, and being all intelligent (omniscience) it brings forth the plan into manifestation.

Divine substance is the material that the divine intelligence uses to mould the plan or desire into manifestation. There is only one universal substance and it does not matter whether it is wood, metal, flesh, rock or vegetation, etc., it is still the same divine substance at a different state of vibration or molecular structure.

The word 'image' (Gen: 1-26) is telling us that we are held in the mind of God. Some think that the word image means shape and this in turn leads to a conception of some divine being somewhere out there external to the self. This incorrect assumption has terrible consequences as it leads us away from the 'oneness of all' to the one sin of the world and that is the 'sense of separation'.

The 'likeness' is that we have exactly the same qualities as God. We are actually the microscopic reflection of the macrocosm. 'As above so below'.

This is part of the meaning of the symbol of the Star of David, which is two triangles, one pointing up and the other pointing down, and note: the two triangles are entwined, not separate.

'The kingdom of heaven is within you' (LK: 17-21). The kingdom is that higher state of consciousness. It is not a physical place, as we would conceive a place to be.

I have talked to people about this and they seem disappointed that heaven is only a state of consciousness. This is because they overlook the fact that we are consciousness and that higher place, that kingdom of heaven within, is our true home or our true state of being.

The other mistake that is made besides the misconception of the word image is that people believe that Genesis 2:7 is a continuation of Genesis 1: 26-28. Genesis 2:7 is explaining the preparation of the physical body (Adam) so that spiritual man (Genesis 1:26-28) can manifest on the physical plane of consciousness.

The rib being taken from Adam (Genesis 2: 21) is symbolic of the fact that all is made from the ONE.

Eve represents the mind, which is the instrument of Consciousness and Intelligence and the body is a reflection of the mind and emotions.

If we try to comprehend God we have to try to comprehend a total entity without size and without boundaries – just a state of being. This state of being is total consciousness and total intelligence. All in ONE, all that IS, is indeed within this consciousness and anything that is bought forward in creation is within the consciousness and manifested by the intelligence.

As I have already explained the laws of the universe apply to the macrocosm just as it does to the microcosm. I will explain the process on our level, but before I do I must say that the purpose of life is to express life, to live life, to create. Life is ever expanding from the very microscopic to the great macrocosm, beyond the great beyond throughout all the different dimensions in endless splendour, and we are that life. We are not the expression of that life, we are that life. The body we have, the emotions we feel, the mind we use, are instruments for that life. Remember this and come to terms with it if you can: *we are not the body, we are not the emotions, we are not the mind, we are life itself, birthless, deathless,* expressing itself through these instruments of expression.

Have you ever wondered at the great variety of life even here on the physical level? The endless designs of the snowflakes, every blade of grass a different design, the very shape of everything in nature designed for the purpose of its survival. It is indeed a world of wonderment and beauty and that same intelligence, that same consciousness that is responsible for this creation is in us. In fact it is us, we are it, there is no separation.

On the physical level we can only explain things by way of comparisons. However, when we talk of things beyond the physical, there are no comparisons, therefore we are lost for words and explanations. This is what Paul meant when he said, "Eye has not seen and ear has not heard the things that await man." (Cor 1. 2:9) Paul was aware, like all enlightened men and women, of the things that are beyond the flesh, but as his mortal self he was subject to the five senses, he was unable to impart its splendour because there is nothing on the physical level to compare it with.

We can look at life on this level of consciousness as a learning exercise in the schoolroom of life. Even though we may not be aware of it, even though we may not understand it, we are steadily, slowly but surely, progressing along the path of enlightenment and yes, we are continually throwing boulders (concepts) on our path as stumbling blocks, but even then we are progressing, albeit ever so slowly.

The different states that we pass through, ie., from a point where we are a total new arrival and subject to all the mistakes we all make, being pushed from pillar to post, stumbling from one problem to another, to being totally in control of our environment because you know that you are your own creator and your own maintainer. We must realise that we are consciousness and intelligence manifesting in substance.

The universal law says that, 'Whatever is in the consciousness is automatically out-pictured by the intelligence.' The male represents consciousness, the female represents intelligence and substance is represented by the offspring. On the physical level it appears as if these are separate, the male or consciousness having a separate body to the female or intelligence. This is only so because of the limitation of our senses. It is still the one life manifesting through all bodies regardless, be they plant, insect, fish, bird, animal, human or angelic beings. There is no separation except in the mind of man.

On the physical level of consciousness, the law works just the same as it does in the macrocosm.

The male (consciousness) puts forward the design or plan (seed) and the female (intelligence) faithfully draws to her the substance needed to complete the direction bringing about the manifestation (child) exactly as the consciousness directs. So we see that the same principle applies right throughout creation. As is now known, it is the male that decides the sex of the child, which must be a blow to all those in the past who would blame the female for not bearing sons.

Each individual male and female is consciousness and intelligence manifesting in a physical body. For example, the male has a female side with the male aspect dominant and the female has a male side with the feminine aspect dominant.

We do, however, have other much finer bodies that allow us to operate on higher levels of consciousness. This is done by all of us, but at the moment, mostly on the unconscious levels. I will speak more of this later.

We should now be able to see that we are here to experience life, but also know that this life is only one of the many different levels of experience. I'm not talking of reincarnation, rather I speak of other levels, other dimensions. Gradually we awaken to our own existence. We become aware THAT WE ARE. This may seem crazy to some. They will say, "Of course I know I am," but there is a difference. The difference is in the 'degree' of awareness and as we progress along this path of awakening we soon find that it is not learning what we are, but rather realising what we are not. After all, we are not the body. How many can truly accept that information at this stage?

There is an intellectual acceptance. But then there is the 'knowing.' As we experience life, we learn to understand the laws of nature and the universal laws. As we do, we gradually take command of our life and our environment. We see many different books now available in regard to the power of positive thinking. Most of them are of little value, reflecting little knowledge of the true self. However, in cases where the information is of value, it is the individual that has to put it into practice. YOU have to do it; no one does it for you, not your friends, your parents, not your preacher, not Jesus – no one but yourself.

The purpose of life is to experience. In effect, the creator experiencing his creation, the playwright taking part in his play.

We humans like to pass the responsibility to another. We would like to think that all we have to do is sing praises and all is well, our seat in heaven is assured. It is true that our seat in heaven is assured but that is regardless of what we do. Hence, you will find that the shepherd will seek every one of his flock until all are home. The shepherd is our true self and the lost lamb is our conscious self still in the unconscious state. It is through experience that the unconsciousness unfolds into spiritual self-awareness. The 'I am that I am.'

Chapter Two

Evolution or creation?

If we are capable of understanding, knowing and accepting that we are not the body, it serves to throw a great deal of light on other unanswered questions. Questions of which I will deal in this chapter. The knowing that we are spirit or consciousness and not the body is like a key to a greater understanding, opening doors to other planes of existence and knowledge. It is not hard to accept, for example, that it is not the body that evolves. This information is like a missing link in the arguments for and against evolution over the years. It is the consciousness that evolves, from the 'whom am I' to the 'I am that I am'.

That is all we will ever really know about ourselves, 'that we are'. Anything outside of that is illusion. The whole plan behind creation and evolution is to evolve from a state of unconscious consciousness to a state of conscious consciousness.

Now I shudder in writing that, knowing full well that you, the reader, will wonder, "What in the blazes is he talking about?" But it is not the truth or knowledge that is complicated, it is we ourselves who tend to complicate things. Unconscious consciousness means a state that is not conscious of the self. The animals, plants, birds, etc. cannot refer to themselves as 'I'. They are under what we call a group consciousness. They function totally on instinct. They eat when hungry, drink when thirsty, rest when tired, propagate in line with the seasons. It is not until the individual point in consciousness, due to the natural expansion of that consciousness over eons of time when it reaches the human state that it refers to itself as 'I'.

If we want to study the habits of lions for example, we do not have to study every lion because each lion will reflect the same habit patterns. Gradually the individual point of consciousness within them will awaken enough to evolve through to human state, more individualised.

Consider the symbol of Sagittarius in the Zodiac, the higher self shooting his arrow to higher planes seeking to free himself of the lower nature. The lower nature is represented by the horse part of his body and the higher self, the man, is aspiring to the higher self. But note they are still joined. The message here is that it is not so much trying to distance oneself from the lower nature as to bring it under the control of the will by way of transmutation.

It is the process called transmutation whereby the creative force which was once expressed as the reactionary instinctive mind (self-preservation) is raised to a higher plane of expression.

I should mention here that the path of man is not the only way for consciousness to evolve.

This other world is the 'elemental world'. This world is written about in many stories of so-called fantasy and looked on as children's stories, probably because the children still maintain the innocence that has not been polluted by the intellect. These are the gnomes, fairies, sylphs, devas, etc. that we have read about as a child and I think it is great that with modern movies, we are again coming to venture into this world – even though the movie-makers tend to go overboard. The path that is taken by these entities is much easier than the human path, although it is much longer, not that that matters.

These little beings, and some not so little, are responsible for attending to nature. We have seen in the Walt Disney movies how they paint the flowers, bring in the seasons. Walt Disney was right on the mark. Much folklore in countries such as Ireland and Germany has many stories of the elemental world.

The devas, who are responsible for 'species' whether they be mineral, plant, insect, fish, bird or animal, are themselves still evolving through the expression and experience of it's manifested species. It is very rare indeed that a human is fortunate enough to come into conscious contact with any of these entities. The reason is that our vibrations are too coarse. We need to be as a child in our attitudes, pure in our motives in order to contact this world. It is the same reason that our planet is so polluted. It's not just because of our total disregard and ignorance of nature by pouring chemicals down the sink, but also because of our attitude to one another. Our thought patterns, words and deeds create coarse vibrations and deter the elementals from their work in nature.

The thought patterns of the individual is shown in the aura. They envelop the individual and in turn affect his/her circumstances, such as health, wealth, and happiness and colours the attitude and response of others to them.

We attract to ourselves in line with our thought patterns. And the same applies to a family. The house itself takes on an aura which will attract to that household circumstances in line with the thought forms of the family as a whole and that makes up the aura.

This applies right up the scale. For example, to towns, cities, countries and finally the whole Earth as the human family as a whole will attract the sum total of the thought forms that envelop our earth.

This in reality is the true source of pollution because it in turn influcnccs materialistic attitudes that have total disregard for the environment.

So, while it is necessary to take part in programs to clean up our waterways and our land the individual can make an even greater contribution by watching their attitudes and motives and thoughts towards themselves and others.

People like to walk into the forests and soak up the atmosphere. This atmosphere should be everywhere. However, while mankind is caught up in his materialistic mania which reflects his inner poverty, ie., void of spiritual qualities, he cannot expect anything but suffering in all areas.

There is really no difference between creation and evolution. The great mistake that is made is in not knowing that it is the consciousness that evolves and that the creationists do not realise that creation is still happening. It is an evolving creation.

The evolutionists argue that everything started with a big bang. There may well have been a big bang but it was a secondary cause not the first cause.

It was simply a method used for creation. But behind the big bank is the consciousness and intelligence that is behind all creation both microscopic and macroscopic.

They do not believe that a great being was behind creation and they are right. At least they are right when considering the separate God that the theologians worship.

But to say there is no divine consciousness and divine intelligence behind creation is a nonsense when we consider the orderly marvels of nature and the universe.

The nonsense that the theologians cling to is the 'world being made in six days' (Earth time). Yet if we read Matthew: 24-34 we can see that time as we know it was not the time that the ancients were referring to.

Matthew: 24-34 says in part, "This generation shall not pass, till all these things be fulfilled."

I think that we can say with confidence when dealing with 'Earth time' that quite a few generations have passed since the Master spoke those words.

Again in (2ndPeter: 3-8), "But beloved be not ignorant of this one thing that one day is with the lord as a thousand years and a thousand years as one day."

So if we remove the concept of a God separate from his creation and talk in terms of universal time rather than Earth time and also by realising that we are not the body and that it is the consciousness that is evolving then the intellectual sparring between the scientist and the theologian can come to rest.

There is no beginning, there is no end. 'I am Alpha and Omega.' God is all there is. How is it possible for God to be infinite if there is even one atom outside of God? Like Shakespeare we can look on it all as a great play on a great stage. We must take on the understanding as Jesus did and realise that 'All are one'. Then we can see that God is the writer of the play, the director, the actors, the audience and even the stage itself.

Consciousness starts off evolution as 'rock consciousness'. Here we have to see that it is by trial and by limitation that the consciousness grows from the state unknowing to knowing. At that first stage, the consciousness now becomes 'aware' of something that it has not known before, even though, yes, it is a limitation, and yes, even though in reality it is an illusion. Consciousness takes on this condition and for the first time 'experiences the limitation of *shape*'. If God is all there is, then he has no shape. So within himself he creates the illusion of creation and by way of evolution, sets out to experience his own creation. Someone once said that, "The dream has been dreamt, it is now being lived."

Try to picture a dull red glow. This represents the unconscious consciousness. This light is only aware of its shape, not heat, cold, hunger, movement or anything but shape. If the rock is broken it does not feel pain. It just takes on the awareness of its new shape. The next step in the evolution is to the mineral kingdom. Here we see shape emphasised in the crystals. What do we do with minerals and precious and semi-precious stones? We shape them, and even at this low stage of evolution it reflects light. So we see that shape is the first principle of evolution.

From there consciousness now expands to the next level of awakening, that of the plant kingdom. Here we see that shape is very important. The very survival of the plant still depends on its designed shape. To catch water, not to catch water, to catch sunlight, not to catch sunlight and so on. However, there is something else now that the consciousness experiences and that is 'movement'. Very limited at first, but the first stage to even greater movement and gradually on and on to independence.

The next stage is the insect kingdom, and as I've already indicated, more independent movement. If the reader is fortunate enough to get hold of a book called *Beyond the Himalayas* by Dr Murdo McDonald Bayne. On one occasion he was going on an expedition in the Himalayas with his friend and an old hermit to find four extremely rare plants, one of which is called Yartsa Gumba. It means summer grass and winter insect. He tells how this plant is a root in the summer and a caterpillar in the winter and when the caterpillar again becomes the root, a flower grows out of its head.

From the insect domain we venture into the fish kingdom. A totally new environment to assimilate. Once again shape and movement play a great part. It is in the fish kingdom that we see very clearly the group consciousness in action. Watch the great schools of fish as they all move as one.

We also see this very clearly in the next step of the path of evolution. Watch the birds as you would watch the fish and see the unity, the oneness. The bird kingdom gives way to the animal kingdom and it is here that we see the first faint glimpses of individuality. The more the animal is associated with the human the more that point in consciousness strives for the individual state.

When the consciousness has reached the human stage it is still saddled with the lower instinctive nature, and as we progress around the wheel of rebirth (the Zodiac) we gradually evolve to a higher state of individual consciousness. But while being individual, we still remain part of the whole.

It takes many incarnations in the human state for the individual consciousness to 'transmute' (not suppress) the instinctive nature and take on the garment of Christ. The Christ is the individualised point of awakened consciousness.

Once we have reached that point, the individual consciousness goes on expanding into limitless cosmic consciousness. Experience is the only avenue of true understanding.

Chapter Three

The make up of man

It is written that man does not live by bread alone. (LK: 4.4). This is yet another way of saying that there is more to man than just the physical side. What I want to do in this chapter is to explain how and when the spirit takes up residence in the physical body, the influence of the planets, the part they play and the difference between free will and destiny.

The birth of a child is no accident, regardless of what we may think. To understand anything to do with creation, evolution or the spiritual level, it is necessary to see things from the cause or spirit through to the manifestation, rather than from here looking back. If we are spirit manifesting in flesh, then it should be obvious that we should see things from the spiritual point of view. The actual preparations of a birth are put into motion long before the actual physical act of inception.

On the other side beyond the flesh these preparation involve the proposed parents, the spiritual helpers and the entity intending to incarnate. They are in turn linked or in touch with higher spiritual entities who are available for wise council as to the phase of spiritual development that the incarnating entity will experience.

The choice of parents is not a hit or miss situation.

Rather, all those involved in families on Earth have been together many times throughout the ages and where one may incarnate as the son in this life it is very likely that this entity was a father or mother or sister or friend or foe to his present Earthly parents and siblings in the past.

The gender of the physical body is chosen by the entity intending to reincarnate in line with experiences that the entity is to experience. The physical vehicle is an in strument through which spirit or an individual point in consciousness experiences the outer states of manifestation for the purpose of what is termed spiritual growth.

However, it is not the only body that we have. There are several planes of consciousness between our true spiritual home and the physical manifestation. These are the mental, the astral (emotional) and the etheric. There are also different levels of these planes as well. Each of these bodies coming from the spiritual state to the physical state gradually become coarser in vibration. They are like relay stations or transformers that gradually tone down the power of the spirit to a level that allows the spirit to manifest on the physical level.

Without these other bodies (besides the ability to function, ie., think, feel, etc.) the physical body would disintegrate as it would not be able to hold the full power of the spirit/self. Imagine putting a thousand watts of power through a sixty-watt bulb. Once the karma of the incarnating entity has been established the time of birth is set in relation to the position of the planets that will ensure that the Earthly life of the entity will be guided along the lines that correspond to the experiences or lessons that he or she has set for themselves.

The entity enters the physical body at the first physical breath which is the precise moment that the planets and signs of the Zodiac are in the position creating an imprint that will guide his or her life in line with the karma chosen for this incarnation. Any physical or mental disability that may manifest (either evident at birth or later in life) is all part of the program that this soul had mapped out for itself with the consultation with those of wisdom before the physical birth.

For those who think that such things are a type of punishment for so called sins of the new arrival or the parents, let me assure you that this is not the case and I make two points here.

1. Such bodies are in big demand from those on the other side because they know that such extra limitations on an already limited manifestation (the physical body) are instrumental in accelerating the spiritual realisation.

2. It is often the case that such bodies are taken on by old souls with the result of not so much for their own spiritual growth but rather as an 'inspiration' to those about them on the physical level. It is their way of serving mankind.

It also needs to be known that qualities and/or talents that have been achieved in past lives are bought forward to a particular incarnation for expression while other talents and qualities lay dormant.

If it is the case as I have written that all is mapped out before birth, then where does free will come into it and does it exist?

We could say that destiny is the mapped out plan of the individual. However, where it is the case that one will arrive at the point of learning that he or she set out to achieve. It must also be remembered that the planets and the Zodiac are in constant motion, which can by virtue of free will bring about a different path or an adjustment. The path, whatever it may be, will lead to the same result. It can be shorter or longer, easier or difficult depending on the individual 'response' to the celestial influences and opportunities that present themselves.

We are constantly by virtue of our thoughts, words, deeds, attitudes and motives modifying our karma every day. We can use the free will to hasten and indeed extend our learning capacity or we can drift and let the stars steer us along the path.

In the final analysis, free will is of the higher self, not the personality.

Chapter Four

Reincarnation and the law of retribution and karma

Reincarnation is another subject that is easy to conceive once we are able to see that we are not the body. However, even with those who believe in reincarnation, there remain many misconceptions. I know that in some countries, reincarnation is used as a scapegoat. The attitude being that it's okay to do this or that now because I can pay for it in a future incarnation.

I have known of people from the west who have gone to India and Tibet expecting to find a Master on every street corner looking for answers in relation to karma as if the great wisdom and knowledge is so well known that almost every person in these countries can teach you. Unfortunately, this is far from the truth and regretfully the majority of these people are caught up in rituals and superstitious jargon and no closer to the truth than anyone else. Both India and Tibet are indeed the custodians of great truth, but it is in the hands of the few, not the many.

I'd like to expand a little more on this subject before proceeding, as there is a great misconception about karma. This word is bandied about mostly as some excuse for someone's plight or circumstances and it is obvious to me that they confuse the law of karma with the law of retribution. For example, some think that if a person is responsible for the death of 100 people that he must be born and suffer death 100 times in similar circumstances to balance out his karma. This kind of thinking is nonsense. The law of retribution is based on the law of attraction. The law of karma is based on the law of love and it is so complex in its nature that it would take an initiate to understand it.

At our stage of development therefore, it is best to leave it and let our consciousness grow to its understanding rather than saddling ourselves with preconceived ideas of it, which in effect, are yet another limitation. To expand on our example; if it were the case that a person was responsible for the death of 100 people, it is up to that individual entity as to how he will balance the scales as it were. He may, for example, come back as a doctor and be responsible for the saving of many lives. There are countless ways to balance the books.

It should be well remembered that the self, our true self, is the greatest task master and if we think that we can, or are even willing, from the other side to overlook our shortcomings, we are only fooling ourselves.

When we enter the physical body the memory of the higher life is shut off, even though we can gain access to it if we know how. Instead, we focus our consciousness through the physical five senses and get caught up in the action and reaction of the physical phenomena and we soon lose sight of the real self.

I'm sure that you have had the experience of being at

the picture theatre and become so engrossed in the movie that all those about you are nonexistent. But we are even worse than this, once we start to try to find our way back to our true source, we do so by looking outside ourselves (still caught up in the senses) with the result one illusion leads to yet another illusion. Our concepts and our preconceived ideas become our dictators and our guides and we become lost in this world of illusion. The blind leading the blind, when all the time we are spirit. We are life. We do not have to search for it, WE ARE IT. We need to become conscious of that fact. The moon represents the conscious and the subconscious mind. The side that we see (the conscious), and the side we do not see (the unconscious).

It is through the subconscious that we have access to all things. We need the cooperation of the subconscious mind. To achieve this we need to understand ourselves, our habit patterns. This requires total honesty and the courage to be honest. We must have the honesty to see ourselves as we really are. Only then can we hope to change things and put our thinking, our attitudes and our motives in tune with the infinite.

Reincarnation allows us the opportunities to come into new bodies and in turn gives us the chance for countless experiences as we make our way from a state of unknowing to a state of knowing. While being born under a particular Zodiac sign, we can take advantage of the particular qualities and principles that are the nature of that sign.

Each sign of the Zodiac represents one of the four elements. Fire, Water, Earth, and Air and in turn these elements represent the qualities of the Spirit, Emotion, Physical and Mental bodies, respectively. We are reborn into the wheel of rebirth (the Zodiac or described in the Bible as a wheel within a wheel (Eze 1:16), over and over until gradually we start to awaken and become aware of our true selves. From a spiritual point of view we are still in the embryo stage and we are growing in awareness so that we will be born into the spiritual world in full consciousness as a Christ Child.

Gradually the circle of the wheel becomes an upward spiral taking advantage of the higher octaves of the signs and the planets until finally we are free of this particular phase of our development (the wheel of rebirth) when we become Christ conscious. All this is taking place automatically even though we are not aware of it.

We are here to experience and express life to the fullest and should not be afraid to live each day with gusto. Unfortunately, we get caught up with our guilt and fears, shackled by the demands of society and not game to step out and live life to the fullest.

We often hear of those who claim to be the reincarnation of some famous person in history. Most times these claims are the result of an overactive ego. These people only serve to cast doubt on the existence of reincarnation itself. The only way one can know of such things as reincarnation is through one's own experiences. All the claims in the world can be argued away. But the experiences we have, those pearls we gather line on line, precept on precept, leave that individual in no doubt. As the old Scot lady said, "Its better felt than telt."

As we experience these things it is wise to learn the

wisdom of silence. There are usually very few people that you can share such things with, at least for now. Sometimes we may not understand fully our experiences, but usually they are enough to make us say to ourselves, "things are not as they seem." It is, of course, the case that people do remember past lives, many have vivid memories of them.

Sometimes there maybe a feeling or an inner recognition as you read about a particular country or era in history. Nothing that you can put your finger on, but there is something.

Memories are shut off for good reason. Do not think for a moment that we were always of good character in our past. History is full of villains. One of them could have been you or me and probably was many times.

It has always been a puzzle to me why the religious leaders deny the existence of reincarnation. They say they are against poverty, racism, greed and fear. One would think that if we were taught the truth of reincarnation based on the principles of Christ, people would have a totally different attitude to our world and each other.

If we knew that we could come back into any circumstances (race, financial, etc.), wouldn't you think that we would strive to make planet Earth a better place so that as we come back again and again things would be better and better instead of worse?

Chapter Five

The creative force

All throughout the ancient stonework, writings and symbols we come across the serpent. This symbol is far more important than the pagan tag that is usually attached to anything other than the accepted modern versions of religion. The scorpion of the Zodiac, the dragon of the eastern religions and the snake or serpent, all represent the creative or sexual force of the body.

This force has its seat of power at the base of the spine which is the chakra or centre that corresponds to the red ray of the colour spectrum. There are seven centres or chakras in the human body, each corresponding to the seven colours of the spectrum. It is up to the individual as to how he or she uses this powerful force. We can use it for procreation, for pleasure through the senses or we can, by certain breathing exercises, raise the serpent up through the centres which in turn awakens us to greater knowledge, awareness and enlightenment. As we gradually start to awaken to the spiritual self, the serpent starts to stir and there is a quickening in our aura.

This stirring is a natural process but we can, by virtue of free will, deliberately quicken the process. The Bible tells us that, "Moses raised the serpent in the desert."(John

3:14). The desert is the lower state of consciousness or lower expression of the sexual force and this is telling us that Moses put into practice certain exercises and fasted in order to raise the force into higher centres – no doubt in order to carry out his mission. The great feats that are recorded of men and women throughout history, whether it be known to them or not, was the result of the raising of this force to the higher centres.

As we go about our lives striving more and more to become a living example of the Christ within us and reflecting the principles of Christ, it is automatic that the serpent fire will rise to higher centres. The knowledge on how to use and raise the force at will is given to those who are ready for it. Being ready for it means that you can be trusted with it for your own good, for the misuse of it can have devastating and long lasting effects on the soul of the individual.

The effect of illegal drugs has the effect of forcing the serpent up the spine through the chakras prematurely. Thus, the individual at first experiences wondrous feelings of ecstasy and sees things of great beauty. However, they fall into the trap of wanting to continue to experiment with such things.

The magnetic fields of the body are reversed and the individual has not the ability to handle such conditions because he has not first prepared himself as a vessel of light, therefore those negative qualities, ie., guilt, fear, uncertainty, anger, etc., that lay hidden in the subconscious mind rise up before him like great beasts with the result the individual ends up going through hell.

As we look through ancient myths and stories to do

with the serpent or dragon it will be noticed that the serpent or dragon are never killed. As shown in the case of St George and the dragon when he subdues the dragon with his lance. In other words, just as I mentioned when referring to the instinctive mind, it is not the slaying that is the aim but rather transmuting its force to the greater or higher expression that is the spiritual.

Jason and the argonauts is another story with the same message. The golden fleece (Aries) is at the top of the tree of life and in his hand is the falcon or eagle which is the higher octave of the Zodiac sign, Scorpio. The dragon, serpent and scorpion have the same meaning. The reason why the Zodiac uses the scorpion as its symbol of the sign ruling the sexual force is that the scorpion is the only creature that kills itself with its own sting. This is typical of what happens when we misuse our creative force. Once the serpent is brought under the control of the will it then becomes the eagle which flies free from the restraints of the physical.

That is why the ancient Egyptian Pharaohs had the serpent at the forehead (under total discipline). On their headgear or on the throne behind them was the eagle, always with the wings outstretched, which symbolised enlightenment.

Medusa on the other hand shows that if the serpent is not under the control of the will and we get caught up in the intellect, which is symbolised by the many unruly snakes she had for hair, then we are subject to the five senses. The five senses should be servants of the will not the master. Perseus killed Medusa by getting her to look into his polished shield as he cut off her head. In other words, as we look into ourselves and see ourselves as we really are, we take up command of our life and put the senses back in their place. This then allows the higher self to free itself from the self-imposed ignorance, symbolised by the release of Pegasus, the winged horse, springing from Medusa's beheaded body.

If we take time to study the ancient myths and stories we can gather great knowledge. The headdress of the American Indian chiefs symbolised the extended aura of an enlightened one. The feathers so fine and colourful are very similar to the aura of the enlightened individual, representing the fine lines of coloured energy flowing outward.

There are many tribes throughout the world that reflect the same meaning. In Australia some have very high headgear with a number of circles on them. This is showing us that they knew about the chakras. It also shows how widespread this knowledge was. It was so natural to all. I look forward to the day when history will be revealed as it was and not as it is written.

The sexual force should never be suppressed. To suppress this force is to make it stronger and it smoulders away prodding at our consciousness, seeking expression. Unless we channel this energy into positive productive activity, it can warp the mind and the emotions, expressing itself through the lower levels of the instinctive mind.

As we see in nature, a seed that is under concrete has the power to grow and crack the concrete. The same principle applies with the fears and guilt that lie in the subconscious mind of the human being. It is the same force that is in the seed in nature. It is just that in one case the force is expressing itself through the seed and in the other case through the human being.

In all the native tribes throughout the globe, rape was unknown. Rape was introduced by the white man. It is a joke that the white man should look down on the Indians and natives as a backward and permissive society. What the white man looked on as permissive was, in effect, an enlightened understanding of the force, and that understanding allowed them to have an orderly society.

The white man on the other hand chose to look on the sexual activity as dirty and immoral and we see the result of it in our society today. The more you suppress the force, the stronger it gets. The false morals of the white man are like the concrete that is constantly giving way to the creative force. Our moralists just keep pouring on the concrete and then wonder why our society is morally bankrupt. The sexual force is a natural force and it is the hiding and putting down of this force that creates the warped attitudes and mentally disturbed people in our society. We must learn to use the sexual force without attaching concepts of good or evil.

To have the serpent in the tree of the knowledge of good and evil leads us away from the path of truth and light. We start to see everything in terms of good and bad. This in turn causes us to go in continuous circles. Just like Samson after his hair was cut; he became a slave to outer forces. The hair is symbolic of the creative force. Once the hair grew back and the force was again channelled properly, he regained his power and was able to bring down the two pillars, which represents duality of the mind. When these natural urges rise up and command our attention, it is bad enough that through our ignorance we suppress these urges, but even worse we attach the thought of evil to them thus magnifying their intensity many times.

The next time the urge arises it is now much stronger and we yet again, while using a greater force suppress it and so it goes. This has been the cycle in the western world over many, many generations with the result our hospitals, gaols and asylums are full and overflowing. When the sexual revolution erupted in the 1960s the pendulum then swung to the other extreme and has continued to create turmoil in all areas of our society.

The so-called sexual revolution is not the cause of the turmoil. The sexual revolution is the result of the ignorance and many generations of suppression of the creative force. The self appointed spiritual leaders of the past, ignorant of its true nature, had no idea how to deal with it or how to advise their followers how to deal with it and therefore set out to suppress it.

It is written, "Resist not evil." (Mt: 3-36). Why would the Master say such a thing? It is because he understood the law and in doing so realised that the more we suppress this form of energy (evil) the stronger it gets.

It is like diseases in our modern society. We actually give them names, an identity, and in doing so we give them power. Just mention the word cancer and see the reaction. Disease, like evil, has no power of its own. Only the power we give it by way of our recognition or fear of them. Knowing this, now we can understand the damage that religion does with all its talk of evil. Creating this great fear of some entity they have created called Satan or the Devil.

Satan is actually the planet Saturn. Saturn in astrological understanding is the great tester. It is the one that puts us through the mill as it were. In a Spiritual sense it is therefore our greatest asset because it is the refining of the spirit that leads to enlightenment.

In the old days (not the ancient days – there is a difference) Saturn in a chart was dreaded and terrible warnings were given to people about the placing of this planet in their natal chart.

The word Devil is simply the not expressing of life to the full as I have already mentioned. Spell the word backwards. The same applies to the word Evil. It is the opposite of life, being too caught up in fears, concepts and guilt instead of seeing these things for what they are and living life as we were meant to. I realise that those in the Bible referred to Satan and the Devil. This was because they had to explain things to the people of those days in the terms that they could comprehend. You would not have been able to explain things in terms of electricity or motor vehicles. You would have to use terms like candles or fire because that was their source of power and light. Or donkeys or carts because that was their mode of transport.

Every time I hear that the Bible is to be rewritten (modernised), I think, "here we go again." I believe they have replaced the word 'heaven' with the word 'sky'. Here we see the sense of separation and ignorance at its height. Now we can say "the kingdom of 'sky' is within you."

God help us.

Chapter Six

GOD

During the 1960s when the influence of eastern religions was pouring into western society, one of the better teachers, Maha Barba, was invited to give a talk and thousands gathered – so the story goes. Maha Barba rose to his feet, the crowd waiting in awe, and he said, "God is love," then he sat down. Now we could say that this man had a great sense of humour. After all, here we have thousands of people who had gathered from far and wide thirsting for words of wisdom and spiritual knowledge and he gets up and says three words, "God is love."

If we were to ask ourselves the question, "What is it that I can be 100 percent sure of?" taking into consideration the fact the we are not the body, the answer is that, "WE ARE", I AM." Anything outside of that, whether it is on the spiritual level or the mental, emotional or physical levels is an illusion.

When we say, "I am," we are really referring to ourselves in the sense of the body rather than the spiritual self; we are directing ourselves more and more into the illusion. The subconscious mind, being ever bombarded with these suggestions of the I AM (in the sense of the false self), starts to bring about the very things that we have referred to ourselves as and to. For example, "I am sick, I am tired," and so on. The 'I' in reality is never sick and the 'I' is never tired. The correct way to say these things is, "My body is tired, my physical body is ill," and so on. You will notice that the Master Jesus did not say, "I am nothing." He said instead, "I of myself am nothing." Here he clearly defines the true self and the false self. For without the Father within us, who is life itself, what would we be but a piece of lifeless matter – not even that – because matter is also an expression of life. We would not exist. Now we have a much clearer understanding of what is meant by the commandment, "Thou shalt not take the Lord thy God name in vain." (Ex: 20-7). The word is, "I AM," God's name is, "I Am." Every time we refer to ourselves as 'I' we should mentally clarify the 'I' we are referring to.

We are all individual expressions of God, with power over all things. We are not truly aware of that fact. Our consciousness has not expanded enough to know, really know, that we are the spirit and not the body. It is only when the scales fall from our eyes and we attain the Christ consciousness that we can say, "I and the Father are ONE."

The story of the prodigal son tells us this. He had separated himself from the father (caught up in the ignorance of his true self) and he went out and ended up living with the pigs (caught up in the world of illusion – the false). It was only when consciousness dawned within him that he realised that he was the son. When he returned to the father (the higher consciousness), did his father chastise him, throw him to some bottomless pit of eternal damnation? No, instead the father was overcome with joy, ordered his servants to kill the fatted calf and clothe him in finery. Every single individual that has been, is and will be, can expect exactly the same treatment when finally we stand free from the shackles of our concepts, theories and emotional turmoil and take on our true birthright, which is the son of God.

God is love. The love I speak of is not the emotional version that we have come to know. This is an expression of love, not love itself. True love is a cohesive force that binds the very universe together. Everyone expresses love at their level of ability. Gradually though, as we progress along the path, we are able to express love to a greater degree. The selfish gives way to the selfless. The selfless grows into the full realisation of the AT-ONE-MENT of all things. It is the sense of separation that puts us in the position of the prodigal son.

There is no separation between the Creator and the created. The latter is a reflection of the former. We can look at it from another point and say, "God is life." The trouble is that we tend to think that we are the body and that 'life is in us'. We must realise that we are that life. The body is an expression of that life. The body is not *us*. We are *not* the body. The body is an instrument that we as the 'life force' use to manifest on this particular plane of consciousness that we call the physical. When the Bible tells us about dying in order to be born again, it is not the physical dying that it is referring to. It is the dying to the misconceptions, the falsehoods, the illusions that we have taken upon ourselves. The Master said, "Let the dead bury the dead." (Mt: 8-22). Surely we do not take this literally unless we are smoking something. It means let the spiritually dead bury the physically dead.

We should never argue about God. When we do we are only throwing backwards and forwards our concepts and misconceptions. The blind lead the blind and they all fall into the ditch. The one sin of the world is the 'sense of separation'. From separation comes fear and out of fear, all its offspring such as hate, jealousy, anger, malice, deceit, greed and suspicion, etc. Because we do not see the self spirit in the other person due to our own ignorance and we only see the body and the shortcomings of others, we therefore register this in our own mind as a threat to us and we react. We are ever reacting to things external to the self, thereby being caught up in illusion. Like when we are at the movies and we get so engrossed in it that our surroundings become totally ignored. We need to stop, see ourselves as we really are and realise what we are doing to ourselves and to each other.

Imagine putting on the virtual reality helmet to play and experience the game and forgetting that you are wearing the helmet. You would spend all of your life 'reacting' to the images on the screen in the helmet.

This is exactly what has happened to all of us incarnate in flesh. We have lost sight of the fact that we are only wearing a physically body to the extent that we think that we are that body.

People go through life wondering if this is right, is that the right thing? Who cares? So, we make a few mistakes, we make a few million mistakes. Who cares? How else can we learn if we do not make mistakes? We learn by experience. Living life, expressing life. After all what is life for if not to be expressed?

The only wrong you can do to put it in a nutshell is to deliberately hurt another in thought, word or deed. The more we realise that All are One, the more difficult it is to deliberately hurt another. As the Master said, "What you do to the least of them, you do to me." (Mt:25-40). What we do to others we do to ourselves.

God is all that there is. All that is, is God. In Him we live and move and have our being. God is not a personality. God is not a concept. GOD IS. I AM

Chapter Seven

Death: the great illusion

I have made the statements that 'we are not the body', 'that all are one', and 'life cannot be separated from life'. This being the case, it now brings into question that which we call 'death' – the ultimate fear that is bred into us from birth. The inevitable experience that we all must face. That blackness, that unknown that is there waiting for all of us. No one escapes. ALL must pass through this veil.

It is no wonder that it is used as a great weapon to strike fear into the hearts and minds of people. On the one hand people are steered from the real truth that they are immortal, birth-less and deathless. On the other they are programmed into believing that death is a reality, that if we worship some far off God that is outside ourselves, some divine personality who separates the sinners from the saints, we may be eligible to get to some place called heaven and be given eternal life.

It is these fears that cause us to be separate from God. In reality we are not separate from God – only in our beliefs and ignorance that are born out of fear. If I were to exchange an old set of clothes for a finer set, should I fear that change, or should I be elated at the thought of a new set of clothes? Death is no different that this. Putting off one set of clothes for a finer set and the great news is that there are no expectations of you. You are life manifesting in a physical body; that is the case whether you are a saint or sinner in the eyes of society.

Those who have set themselves up as the representatives of God do a great injustice to their fellow man by creating this childish fear in their hearts and it is these fears that are the stumbling blocks along the path of truth and light. Death is the great illusion.

The 23rdPsalm in part says, "Yea, though I walk through the valley of the shadow of death, I will fear no evil." The word 'shadow' is the key word – 'shadow of death'. The shadow of anything is not real; it is only a shadow. The Bible talks often about death. That is true, but it is not death, as the theologians would have you believe.

For example, the Bible says that you must be born again. Some think that this is dying and then one day jumping up out of the grave all enlightened. Others think that it is giving up our worldly (sinful) activities and accepting some orthodox religion thereby being saved and guaranteed eternal life as if religion has some kind of patent on God, truth or Christ.

To be 'born again' is to die to the old self as we are, perhaps the materialistic self or the selfish self, and take on the Christ self or the higher self. In other words the Christ self is able to manifest its principles through you, unhindered. This is not just a case of saying, "I accept Jesus as my Lord and Saviour', going to church every Sunday and being what society believes is a 'good citizen', which often means being like a robot living the rules that the church has decided is the way to live.

Little do they know, it is the *theories* and *concepts* of the mind that are the very things that are the usurper of the higher self or the Christ self. The Christ self cannot manifest through us if our mind is cluttered with all our concepts. These are the demons; these are the offspring of the sense of separation (the sin of the world). Thou shalt have no other Gods before me, (Ex: 20-3). These are the things that cause death, but it is the spiritual death that it speaks of.

We should see now that we are spiritually dead, caught up in the illusions of the mind, the concepts. God is not a concept. People do not worship God. They worship their concept of God. God is not a personality.

Why do you think that Jesus said, "I of myself, can do nothing, (Jn:5-30). Here, he is putting the intellect in its place, as the servant not the master, and recognising the higher inner self and therefore allowing it to do its work. But what do we do? We have all these theories and concepts about God and ourselves that clutter the mind and do not let access of God or the higher self to manifest through us. Therefore, we remain in ignorance and be spiritually *dead*. We must achieve the realisation that we *are* eternal. We do not have to earn it. *We are eternal, now*.

We are spirit manifesting in a vehicle (the body) that we have designed so that we as spirit can manifest on the physical level of consciousness for our own self-expression and spiritual growth. When we take up residence in the physical body we become subject to the *senses* of the body. It is through these senses that we can *experience* the physical world. We can hear it, see it, smell it, taste it and feel it. Without being subject to the senses this world would not exist. It only exists because we are *conscious* of it. We are only conscious of it because we are consciousness. The body only has life because we as consciousness are presently manifesting in the body thereby giving it life. Hence, God (life) breathed into man (the body) the breath of Life and He (God) becomes a living soul, (Gen:2-7). Or to put it another way, God, (life or consciousness) becomes manifested in flesh on the material plane of consciousness.

What I have just said will come easy to some, yet others will have to read it over and over in order to grasp it. Only then by way of this knowledge can you hope to see that death is an illusion. Indeed, it takes faith and great courage to be able to see and believe this. After all, you are flying in the face of the more accepted orthodox. You feel alone and out of it so to speak. It is true that the path is a lonely one. However, no one can walk it for you,

The loneliness that you may feel is in itself an illusion. For in reality, there are by far more with you, encouraging you, than are against you. It is the unseen that is the real and the seen that is the illusion. Remember that what we see through the senses is subject to the limitation of the senses. For example, the physical eyes can only function at around 500 billion vibrations per second. Yet we know that there are things able to be seen at vibrations much higher than this. Animals can see things that we cannot. This is because the animal, being an expression of group consciousness, is closely linked with nature.

Our ears can only pick up vibrations between 16 to 32,768 vibrations per second. Yet there are sounds that exist beyond these levels.

So there are other finer worlds or planes of existence than that of the physical and for these levels we have finer bodies so that we as consciousness can also function on those planes. This can be consciously achieved while we still *have* a physical body, but not while we believe that we *are* the body. It is this belief that is the very thing that binds us to the physical level.

There is no need to worry or fear that we may not achieve the higher self or consciousness. It is true that we are IT, but the difference is that we need to *realise* that we are IT. This realisation is a natural process; no one misses out no matter how materialistic we may be. And yes, you can say, "Oh well, I'll just sit back, enjoy life, and let it happen." What we tend to do instead because of our sense of separation is to become insecure in ourselves, which then brings about possessiveness. This then brings about the fear of losing that which we conceive as being secure or what represents our securities with the result that we are continually on the defensive, reacting to things and conditions external to the self.

We need to constantly keep watch and stand porter at the door of the mind watching every thought and turning away those born of separation and ignorance, for it is the intellect that is the greatest trap that the soul can enter. As we stand porter, we allow the higher Christ self to spread the light of truth, expanding our consciousness, allowing ourselves to stop hitting our head against the headstones of misconceptions, and we are able to walk the path of enlightenment in our right mind, which is the Christ mind.

Paul said, "Let this mind be in you, which was also in Christ Jesus." (Phil 2:5).

Dr Mac tells us that the awakening comes in two stages. First there is a *recognition* of that higher state of self. Then there is the *realisation* of our AT-ONE-NESS with God.

These two steps are along the way on the path and we can never know at what stage we are at. Those who may seem righteous may not be so, and those who seem sinners may not be so. To judge is to reveal that we are still caught up in ignorance.

It should be known that we are totally different people or entities when we are on the other side. On the other side we are our true selves with the mask of the limitations of the physical senses and intellect removed. In reality we are all great spiritual beings.

We choose to come into the flesh for our own spiritual development. It is for our expansion of the awareness of our true state that is the goal.

We do this by getting caught up in the illusions of the world's limitations in order to allow for the growth of our awareness of our true selves. Words become very inadequate when trying to explain this area, but it is by becoming aware of what we are not that allows us to realise that *we are*.

We tend to think in terms of age and the years that

we have left, because we are ignorant of the fact that the so-called death is only a temporary transition from this physical state until we once again reincarnate (which we do countless times) to continue our spiritual journey. We should forget the limitation of thinking of a single lifetime and try to realise that we have eternity to achieve our goals. This tends to lift a great burden from our hearts and foster that great quality of patience. It is the little things in life such as our fears, anger and general reactions to the outside world that hinder our awakening, not some Devil or Satan that is only the imagination of the fear-mongers. The belief in these things steer you away from realising that the fault lies within ourselves and not the cause of some external evil force. Once we can see this we can immediately start to work on ourselves and strive to express the qualities of the Christ self rather than the false self that is caught up in superstitions and ignorance.

Because of these states, people find themselves constantly wrestling with their conscience. Some become so frustrated that they tend to kill off the conscience in desperation, usually to save sanity. They go from pillar to post in their minds on that endless merry-go-round of good and evil. There is the conscience, that still small voice that is our higher self, and then there is the acquired conscience that is the result of our programming by parents and society as they try to instil fear into us and fill our minds with stupid superstitions. I know that they do these things out of concern for us, trying to warn us of all the dangers in life. They themselves went through the same programming and do not know any better. Such is our society, so void of truth and understanding.

Quite often you will find, as we all do, that we fail to live up to our principles. The one thing that we must never do when this happens is to become frustrated or feel guilty. Remember, it is the feeling of guilt and frustration that in turn blocks the higher expression of the true self. Some may say that it's natural for murderers, for example, to feel guilty. They would be angry if the murderer did not feel guilt of his deed.

This may be true, but what I'm trying to say is that if we knew how to deal with all the guilt, fears and inferior complexes that tend to build up over many years, and if we were to learn how to *transmute* them rather than *suppress* them, then there would not have been a crime in the first place.

Guilt is a reaction that fosters reaction and more times than not the individual ends up in more trouble. Each experience in life is like a little death, where we die to an old concept, replaced by the realisation (hopefully) that it was only a concept and now we are free of it. However, most times we trade one concept for another concept.

Chapter Eight

Our ability to leave the body

A figment of imagination? Can it really be done? How many individuals have had experiences that they cannot explain – that they dare not speak about for fear of ridicule or having their sanity questioned? It is amazing how much energy is spent trying to maintain the ignorance of our society, as if knowledge was some kind of threat. Well, the time is now when things, as they are, will be seen as they are. Nothing will be hidden.

There is so much knowledge that is to be realised, but we must adjust to knowledge as it is rather than trying to have knowledge conform to our limited concepts. We need to open our minds and not be afraid to step out and think for ourselves. To conform with due consideration, is one thing. To conform out of sheer habit yet another.

In the past, anything that was not understood was put in the evil basket. When radio was first invented, for example, it was looked on as the voice of the Devil. It is no wonder that things like astral travel caused great suspicion and fear.

Have you ever had the sensation of floating while you were in bed or asleep? Found that you were frozen stiff and couldn't move a muscle in the middle of the night?

Your body is asleep, yet you are still awake? You have visited a place for the first time yet you have somehow been there before? Well, you are not alone. These are normal and natural experiences that most of us have at sometime during our life. Most put these experiences aside in the 'just one of those things' basket. Most children experience astral travel as a matter of course. It is so common to them that they do not realise that it is not really known or accepted in society.

Gradually, as we grow older, we become more and more immersed in the physical world and we steadily lose sight of that other subtle world that was so familiar to us. Some, at a tender age, even have a little friend (invisible to everyone else) who is so real to that little person that the physical surroundings fade into insignificance. According to our society it is just a phase the child is going through or it is a supplement to something that is missing in the child's life.

Previously, I explained the make up of man. We have got to realise that we are spirit and not the body. Once we can see this, then things like astral travel become a natural understanding and not something that is considered far out or evil. We are totally free once we transcend our limited concepts and realise our abilities. On the other end of the spectrum there are those who have exploited the upsurge of interest in astral travel. It's marvellous, the moment there is a new interest or the surfacing of information, immediately we have all these 'experts' writing books and coming up with the methods of how to attain them. How sad it is that we witness the inner poverty of humanity totally starved of truth, groping around here and there spurred on by an inner discontent.

We anguish on the inner while out of pure frustration we turn more and more to lose ourselves in the physical. We want to be constantly entertained to keep our attention wandering so that we do not see ourselves as we are – a pauper amidst the universal riches of our true being.

The art of leaving the body revolves around the training of the subconscious mind. The subconscious mind is like a child and is indeed a child. It needs to be encouraged as we would a child, firing the enthusiasm, the inquisitiveness, the mystery. Knowing this, we see how necessary it is to free ourselves from the misconceptions, fears and all the things that serve to assault the purity of a child-like mind.

Allow yourselves to return to the splendour of daydreaming, pondering and imagining. Do we ever need to wonder why our joints and bones seize with age when we have limited and concrete attitudes and concepts? "As you think, so you are." Whatever is in the mind or the emotions will reflect on the physical body, for the body is the sounding board of the mind and the emotions. It is the limitations we place upon ourselves that submerge the innocence of the true self.

When we come to know of and believe in things like astral travel and we try to experience it, there is all this accumulated rubbish that we first must clear away. To enlighten (unclutter) the mind, to calm the emotions, allows for the child to be reborn in the manger of simplicity. The moment that we consciously start to walk the path of truth and light, those who are our spiritual companions and guides are able to help us in earnest. They can only help us to the degree that *we* allow. Do you think it matters if we know little or nothing of the great mysteries of life? In truth, it matters very little. In fact, not to know is more of an asset because anything that we think we know other than what we ourselves have experienced is a concept, a stumbling block. We block the natural working of nature, whether it is on the physical, mental or emotional levels, because of concepts.

For me to tell you what you will experience when you leave the body only serves to create a preconceived idea of what it is like and this alone can distort and hinder a true experience for you. It is far better that I give you hints on how to attain the leaving of the body.

Each will experience this in their own way and while it is an aid in attaining the goal of self-realisation, remember, it is not the goal itself. It is but a step. Also remember that when you start to apply yourself to these things that you come directly under the exactness of the divine law. These laws are simple yet they are exacting. The qualities of self-discipline, honesty, and selflessness are now needed as your armour against the tests that shall beset you. Therefore, watch your motives. Know that the motive is always greater than the deed. The 'why' you do something rather than 'what' you do.

It is understandable and yes, permissible to experiment with astral travel. For example, you may find yourself away from the physical body, realising that you are out of the body. This can bring a sense of fear or a great sense of excitement and anticipation. You can practice walking through walls, you can try flying or you can call on your guides. Most times though, you will know within yourself what you must do, and this is usually in line with your development.

While it is necessary to bring to your attention the presence of the laws, I do not mean to stifle the fun-loving Peter Pan in each of us. There are a great many adventures that can be experienced away from the physical vehicle and a great deal of learning can be obtained as well. You can even visit higher levels of consciousness and, even though I myself have not yet had the privilege, I do know of those who have been in the presence of the Master himself while away from the body.

Such experiences are your pearls, so heed the advice that is given and, "cast not your pearls before swine."(Mt:7-6). In other words, realise that there are very few about you who you can share such experiences with. Most will ridicule you but, as we will see, this attitude will soon change, as the awareness of individuals and humanity as a whole is elevated to a higher octave of understanding.

Remember, it is the subconscious mind that is the key. You must gain its cooperation. To help you with this, the following simple exercises will help you.

As you go about your day, stop and look around you. Take note of where you are and what you are doing. Are you in the astral or the physical body? The subconscious mind loves habit patterns and by doing this exercise daily and periodically, it is quite possible that by way of habit one night when you are asleep, and unconsciously in the astral, that you will do this exercise, which will lead to you realising that you are out of the body.

Write down all your dreams no matter how trivial. Put them down exactly as they happened, not forgetting to describe the feelings in the dream. Then, as time passes and you read over them, it helps to train the subconscious mind to remember. In this way a great deal of information is gathered which helps you in your daily life.

Learn to relax. Dr Mac says that the art of relaxation is a science and gives the following instructions in his book. *How to Relax and Revitalise Yourself.*

Place your body on a firm mattress, pillow supporting the head and shoulders, pillow under the knees, feet about half a metre apart, your arms by your side and hands resting on the groin. Breathe in and as you exhale, let your body relax.

Talk to your body, ie., "Legs and arms relax, relax, let go, let go." The limbs must be the first to relax as the rest of the body cannot relax if the limbs are not relaxed. Now tell your chest muscles to relax, let go. Now the vertebrae, then the stomach muscles, shoulders, facial muscles, eyes, ears and so on. Only half an hour a day will see a big improvement and you will see results in your physical health as well. You will feel full of zest and develop a positive attitude towards your surroundings. I will repeat this information on relaxation later.

It may take a while to get results on the astral for some. Do not get despondent. When you do start this journey, never be afraid. Fear is your greatest enemy. You cannot lose your body, you always return to it. No one can enter it while you're gone. That would be against divine law. Keep your thoughts and aspirations high, your motives pure and you can do no wrong.

The greatest asset to the leaving of the body lies in the enthusiasm. The excitement, anticipation and 'the can't wait to get there' approach. The ability to rekindle that childhood excitement is of great benefit and a 'key' to this exhilarating adventure.

A light meal, such as salad is desirable before retiring. This is good advice in regard to general health but it also does assist when training to achieve the leaving of the body.

Chapter Nine

Preparing the temple

When taking into consideration the function of the physical body, we understand that the mind and emotions play the greater part in maintaining health. The physical body is the 'sounding board' of the mind and emotions.

It is the quality of our thoughts, positive or negative and our emotional reactions that find expression on the physical level of manifestation reflecting through the organs and functions of the body that decide our state of health on all levels.

It must be remembered that spirit is always perfect. The true self in reality is totally unaffected by what goes on in the mind and emotions and does not suffer disease, unlike the physical body. While spirit maintains and gives life to the body, the discord and the inharmonious that can apply to the mental and emotional bodies are the result of the individual consciousness being at the stage of being unaware of its true nature and birthright, thus becoming caught up in the illusionary world and a continuos battle rages on the mental and emotional levels in their reactions to things external to the self, thereby manifesting conditions we call disease in mind and body.

A vicious cycle is set up whereby it is the case that the

initial cause of a condition starts in the mind, this in turn attracts the intake of foods of high acid contents and poor eating habits which poisons the system. This then sets up an agitation that irritates the nerves and glands leading to nervous irritability creating a form of insanity. The mind and emotions in such conditions (of our own making) continue to react even more so due to these irritations and so the cycle continues.

The only way the Christ self (your true self) can manifest on Earth is for the instruments of mind, emotions and body to become a fit and proper place for the Christ to abide. This is demonstrated in the Bible story when Christ chased out the money changers from the temple.

The physical body is the temple unmade by hands. The money changers are all the concepts, fears, greed and guilt, etc. that take up the space and are the usurper of the spirit. Jesus was cleaning up his temple.

The trick now is to break this cycle or circle. We know that a circle has no beginning and no end. So where do we start? It is true that the initial 'cause' of our conditions lie in the mind and emotions.

It is also true that we should treat the cause rather than the effects. We should remember, however, that the body conditions are creating negative influences for the mind and emotions, perpetuating the irritations and negativities.

The nerves and glands are polluted and it becomes necessary therefore to attend to cleaning up the body as an initial first step, so that the state of the instruments of the mind (nerve endings, glands, etc.) are freed up, thereby starting the process of dealing with the mental and emotional causes.

Once we have cleaned out the physical body we then need to make sure that we 'maintain' the body by way of good natural foods, proper hygiene, sensible exercise and the intake of plenty of pure water.

Dr Mac says that, "The majority of people are over fed and undernourished."

An understanding of the misuse of the way we use our mind is by using the slide projector as an example.

The projector represents the mind. The light focused through the projector is spirit or consciousness and the screen is the external manifested life. The slides would represent our needs or desires we wish to manifest.

The correct working with the universal law is that in our mind's eye we plan in every detail what we desire, and when it is complete we place the slide in front of the light, ie., We give it light through 'gazing' upon the plan while infusing it with emotion and then 'allowing' the light to bring forth our plan, desire or need.

For those who can understand. The universal law states that, "The motive is the key, the emotion is the power." And the universal law also says that, "Whatever is in the conscious is automatically out-pictured by the intelligence."

The main problem is that man tends to overlook the simplicity of the process of manifestation and therefore works by the sweat of his brow.

We think that we have to be there doing things and find it hard to let go and let God. With the result that instead of placing the one slide into the projector that is our plan or desire, we add to it other slides which represent our lack of faith, anxiousness, worry, fear and so on with the result that the manifestation on the screen of life, rather than a beautiful picture (complete manifestation of our desire or plan) is a conglomeration of confusion and half results.

Dr Mac says in his Chapter on 'The subtle Power of Emotion' in his book *How to Relax and Revitalise Yourself* (p.31-32), "All emotions and desires are mental currents. There are two different kinds of mental currents although only one force underlies both. We have the current that acts against us and the current that acts in our favour.

'There is no limit to the number of emotions, let us name some: impatience, anger, hate, indulgence, jealousy, egotism, fear, selfishness, approbation, vanity, terror, dread, dismay, panic and fright, etc. These act against us.

"Then there is the great emotion that acts in our favour, 'love'. Little do we know that the body is the sounding board for all the emotions and according to their intensity so we are affected. Think of your organs making a certain sound when aroused by any of these emotions. Your heart beats faster, your breathing apparatus is checked, your sweat glands pour out liquid, your stomach turns over, your intestines rumble and your tear glands weep. If all these vibrations were to be heard by the ear it would cause a discord beyond our imagination. Yet these organs really call out in vain for relief."

CHAPTER TEN

Four gateways to good health

Our first step in the cleaning out the physical body is to understand the four functions of the body where waste in one form or another is eliminated. These four areas are the kidneys, skin, lungs and the bowels.

If any one of these functions is not working the stress load is then placed on the other outlets. Usually if the skin is not working properly then the kidneys are affected and when the kidneys are affected, the skin is affected in both colour and odour.

When the bowels are not functioning correctly then it is usually the lungs that suffer initially then the whole system. The intelligence in the body will do all it can to assist and overcome any problem that presents itself in the body. It will discard of the waste in any way it can so as to keep the vital organs going and will place waste in areas such as the joint areas, which later in life crystallise and we end up with arthritis.

The importance of keeping the four gates open and in good working order cannot be over-emphasised and throughout this section I will be giving information and handy hints on how to first achieve and then maintain our blood and body that is toxin free.

The intake of plenty of pure water is a vital step in this program. Water will take its own weight in waste out of the body. However, it seems these days the only time we tend to drink water is when we pop a pill.

Soft drink, tea, coffee and alcohol have unfortunately replaced water as our fluid intake much to the detriment of our health. Not only is the water intake itself important but also the *way* we drink it can boost the value of it many times.

I will digress here for a moment to share with you what Dr Mac tells us in relation of the proper drinking of water, proper breathing and proper eating.

Have you ever wondered how the nervous system gets its nourishment? Well, one of the important advantages of eating fresh foods as opposed to prepared foods (including frozen, tinned, dried, etc.) and drinking fresh water that has not been contaminated by sugar and chemicals. Breathing fresh air is the presence of prana or vital energy, which is the very life force that maintains manifested life. It stands to reason that if we can take in this life force in greater quantities then it will be of great advantage to our health and wellbeing.

If we were to leave an apple and an avocado out on the bench we would find that in a day or two the avocado will go rotten but the apple, although not at its best, will still be quite okay to eat. This is because the dissipation of the prana from the avocado is quicker than from the apple.

We find this right across the food spectrum as some foods will keep longer than others. But in all cases it is the presence of the prana or vital energy that maintains the food value of any food item.

Knowing this then we can now appreciate the value of fresh food. It is also interesting and rewarding to know how we can consciously extract the maximum energy from our fresh foods.

In the teeth, gums and tongue there are tiny instruments whose job it is to extract this vital energy from our foods and water and distribute it to the nervous system.

As we chew our food we are in turn releasing this vital energy and this is absorbed and used by the nervous system. When we start to consider the types of foods we eat in our modern world, is it any wonder why there are so many nervous disorders?

So it is not only what we eat and drink but also *how* we eat and drink. Not only are we eating denatured foods (ie., devoid of the freshness and vital energy) but also we usually bolt our foods taking in a mouthful, chewing it a few times and then washing it down with a beer, wine, tea or coffee. The same applies to water when we do drink it; usually, we gulp it down while on the run.

Now we see the importance of masticating our foods properly. Not just to assist the digestion but to get full advantage of the prana that is available to us. Food should be thoroughly masticated and water should be sipped slowly and held in the mouth for a moment before swallowing. The breathing in of fresh air in tune with nature is yet another access to pure prana. I will cover the importance of breathing further on.

Keeping in mind that we are consciousness and

intelligence manifesting in substance we can now take advantage of yet another vital handy hint in relation to the intake of prana. It is this: our very *awareness* of the process of our intake of prana while we are eating or drinking serves to boost its energy value even further to be of greater benefit to us.

This is why the Buddhists never speak while they are eating. Instead they are concentrating on the process going on while they are taking in sustenance, thereby taking full advantage of what nature supplies for our health and wellbeing. Einstein once said that the energy in a single blade of grass could power the Queen Mary around the world until it rusted out.

I believe that it was the prana that he was referring to, but the trick is how to extract this energy? Well, from the point of view of food intake we now have the answer.

In the time that now approaches we need to become aware of the subtle energies that are about us and our bodies need to become finer instruments in order to be in line with these energies. Otherwise it is like the present physical body coming into contact with radioactive material.

The more we apply our selves to the Christ principles in our daily life, the more our vibrations are raised in line with the energies of the incoming age.

With the eating habits that now apply in the modern world, is it any wonder why our hospitals are full to capacity, our operation waiting lists a mile long and our national medical bill going through the roof?

It is said that the physical body is 75 percent water. This information alone points to the importance of drinking plenty of water. It allows the body to flush the toxins and waste out of the body and keeps us in good health. Constipation is without doubt a major cause of illness. Poor eating habits, not enough fluid, too much tea and coffee, not enough exercise and lack of sleep are some of the causes of constipation. From experience I can say that the main cause of the common cold and the yearly suffering of influenza is constipation.

For those who will say that they are the other way inclined, ie., always running to the toilet. I say that this to is also a form of constipation. Dr Mac says never go four to five days without a good bowel movement.

The answer is of course a change in our life style. Correcting our living habits and diet. Colonic irrigation every three months is recommended. You can do it yourself by injecting two pints of warm water containing a teaspoon of bicarbonate of soda and a teaspoon of glycerine.

The aim should be for natural movement with the initial cleaning out process using the suggested enemas. Fruit and vegetable juices and pure water are of great all-round benefit to the body.

Another part of the body that needs an occasional rest and cleaning is the digestive system. This is best achieved first thing in the morning by drinking the juice of one normal sized lemon and three glasses of warm water.

I usually put the juice of half the lemon in the first glass, the second half of the lemon in the second glass followed by the third glass of warm water (blood heat). Then lie on your bed with a pillow under your buttocks and move your stomach up and down. This will cause the fluid that you have just taken to move around like the action of a washing machine and the lemon juice cuts the built up slime from walls of the stomach, thus freshening it up and allowing the digestive juices to flow.

When the reader begins this process he or she may initially feel a little nauseous, however, with practice and after you gradually get rid of the bulk of the waste you will experience a spark and the zest for life starts to return. After all, is it not said that the stomach is the seat of happiness?

To maintain the digestive system in good working order we should masticate our foods properly, drink healthy fluids in the manner that I have suggested, miss a meal occasionally (fasting one day a week or fortnight is better), and drink fluids half an hour before and after the meal. Drinking with a meal weakens the digestive juices. Relax before, during and after eating and get adequate rest. Eat your starch and protein foods separately because together they create an acid in the stomach. Starch foods should be taken in the middle of the day, as they require physical activity or exercise to digest.

Some health advisers suggest a very high protein diet. The healthy body consists of 18 percent protein, and when taking in protein there needs to be plenty of oxygen, and hydrogen-bearing foods and these you get in juicy vegetables and juicy fruits. Fruit taken with meat is very valuable indeed. (Dr Mac's *Heal Yourself* pages 151-152).

The intake of healthy fluids will automatically start to improve any problems with the kidneys and the skin.

The fluids will flush both these organs and they will respond immediately. An occasional sauna and dry skin brushing each morning will do wonders for the skin. Most, if not all skin conditions, can be illuminated through this healthy approach.

Skin brushing is done each morning with a stiff scrubbing brush, in a circular motion all over the body. At first it may feel a bit hard on the skin but before too long you will find yourself brushing with great vigour and wanting a stiffer brush. It is best to change the brush after each fortnight.

Skin eruptions of teenagers are mostly due to digestive disorder. They will find that the internal stomach bath each morning, plenty of healthy fluid intake along with a healthy diet will deal with this situation to their satisfaction.

Two good foods to assist cleaning out the kidneys are asparagus and cauliflower.

The other large organ that needs attention is the liver. This organ is said to be the seat of the desire body.

When the science of astrology is once again accepted, especially in relation to diagnosis, then we come to understand that each sign of the Zodiac and each planet is represented in the physical body by an organ or a function. The liver is a representation of Jupiter (our largest planet). The nature of Jupiter is to do with expansion. If a person has a badly placed or/and aspected Jupiter in their natal chart then they need to watch things like over-eating because both the weight and the liver will suffer.

Sometimes we may feel a little lethargic and sluggish.

This is due to the liver being out of order. Dr Mac tells us that the best way to treat the liver is with fresh tomato juice. Some people say that tomatoes do not agree with them. But this is because the liver is not in working order. He suggests that tomatoes should be taken in small quantities and increased until the liver is getting back to normal. Tomatoes contain Calomel, which absorbs the toxins in the Liver.

Then there is the simple exercise that stimulates the liver from its sluggish state. Stand erect bend back and to the left. While in this position give the liver area a good slapping with the open hand.

At the end of this book I will include a New Start Regime which I have put together and used myself over the years. This is based on the teachings and information that I have gained from Dr Mac. I stress again when seeking good health to make sure there is a large intake of pure water and healthy fluids.

If we break the laws of nature, it will make us pay. If we work with nature, it will in turn assist us in all areas of our life.

Chapter Eleven

The breath of life

"And the Lord God formed man of the dust of the ground, and breathed into his nostrils the 'breath of life'; and man become a living soul." (Gen 2:7).

We can go for some days without food, we can even go for sometime without water, but without the breath, only minutes. If we were to think about this, we soon come to realise how important it is to keep the system flowing in order to continually get rid of the toxins in the body.

The body is building up and tearing down at a very active rate as the blood literally rushes throughout the body delivering the vital oxygen and nutrients and carrying away the waste and toxins. In a 24-hour period it is said that 20,000 litres of blood flow through the body.

The breathing is in constant motion and nature has even supplied an automatic breath stimulator that saves us the trouble of having to remember to breathe. Unfortunately, the greater percentage of people today do not know how to breathe properly and this is reflected in the numbers of those suffering some type of chest problem such as asthma, bronchitis and now tuberculosis.

There are three types of breathing that seem to apply today. They are diaphragmatic breathing, intercostal breathing and clavicular breathing. Each one of these are harmful, in particular the last two. Intercostal breathing is breathing from the mid chest. Clavicular breathing is only using the top section of the lungs (shallow breathing).

What is needed is to combine the three in one flowing movement, taking in the air through the nose that slightly extends the abdomen then travels up filling the mid section. The breath is then held for a moment. This has two effects.

1. It sends air up to the top lobes of the lungs and the clavicular area is energised.
2. By holding the breath for a moment the prana is absorbed and distributed to the nervous system.

The actual cause of asthma is incorrect breathing and it is the lack of oxygen to the upper lobes that tends to be the area of the majority of chest troubles.

As an early morning exercise, especially at sunrise, stand or sit straight but relaxed, arms by your side. As you take in the breath raise your arms and on completion of the breath intake raise your arms above your head. While holding the breath let the arms drop back loosely by your side. This will shoot the oxygen into your lungs to the upper section of your chest. Hold the breath for as long as possible then exhale vigorously, expelling all the air. Do this three times each morning building to six times per morning, expanding to doing it also before retiring for the night. This has the effect of expelling the waste from the body through the lungs. Sunrise is the best part of the day to get quality prana, when the first rays of the sun invades our atmosphere. However, remember that this living force is always all around and through us.

Once you can comfortably do the six then add the next step.

When you drop your arms, while still holding the breath, bring the arms up in front of you and throw them backwards and side ways.

Do this about three times while holding the breath then let the arms return to your side then exhale vigorously. This has the effect of expanding the chest capacity.

Once this exercise becomes natural for you, you then can go a step further. This is to do with the 'conscious' intake of the prana.

As you breath in imagine that you are breathing in life itself; hold the breath then as you exhale imagine that it is filling and healing your whole being.

This is truly breathing in tune with nature. What a wonderful thing nature is. To be at one with nature is to live by its laws and realise that we are one with nature.

We can actually breath away our problems. Oxygen is a positive force that invades our being (if we allow it) and disperses the negative conditions and our life takes on our true birthright of health, wealth and happiness.

I can not over-emphasise the importance of this subject. If proper breathing techniques were taught in our schools then the crime rate and the hospital waiting list would decrease dramatically overnight. I recommend that you start with the exercises that I have given at the end of the book as soon as possible and see the result for yourselves.

These exercises will refer to 'a natural breath'. It is important to know how to breathe properly. I did touch on this point earlier but it is necessary due to its importance in our life and health that the reader knows how to experience a complete natural breath.

The reason why we should breathe in through the nose is that the nose is richly supplied with blood in the mucous membranes, which serves to heat the incoming air to blood temperature so that we do not have cold air going to hot lungs.

Also, we have natural dust catchers that line the nostril passage and serve to catch any dust or bacteria that may be in the air. When we breathe out through the nose the carbon dioxide kills any bacteria and takes with it the impurities that have been gathered from the air during inhaling. Exhaling through the mouth at times such as the breathing exercises is okay and serves to expel more of the body waste.

The complete breath is when we inhale and the diaphragm area expands a little, then the intercostal area and then up to the clavicular area. It is an upward movement of the air rather than just breathing at the mid and top area of the lungs. Dr Mac explains that the proper breath also serves to have the diaphragm massage the stomach.

Everyone can benefit from proper breathing. From those who suffer any type of respiratory complaint to those who are seekers of truth.

Breath is life.

Chapter Twelve

Stand porter at the door of the mind

Now that we have cleaned out the physical body, freeing up the nerve endings, organs and blood of toxins and waste, we can turn our attention to the area of First Cause.

The story of Adam and Eve, when understood, is not a story of male and female, but rather of body (Adam) and mind (Eve).

The reader will notice that in Genesis 1:27, God created man in his own *image* He created male and female.

It was not until some 11 verses later (Genesis 2:7) that he formed man out of the dust of the ground.

Here we see the difference between the spiritual man (male and female) and the actual physical body that is prepared for them on this level of consciousness.

The reason that I have emphasised the word 'image' is that it pertains to the mind the same as the word knowledge as in the 'Tree of the Knowledge' of good and evil. Also, it does not say 'made in his *shape*'. These points are very important when one is trying to understand that we are spirit and not the body.

Once Eve partakes of the fruit of the Tree of the Knowledge of good and evil then that is the point that we get caught up in the intellect and it is the intellect that is the greatest trap that the human soul can enter into.

The intellect has its seat in the brain. The human brain is shaped like a tree and its branches are the sensory nervous system, which are the five senses, sometimes referred to as 'the Satan of the Senses'.

The young soul gets caught up in this web of illusion (ie., things external to the self) and continues to react to the outer stimulus, thereby losing sight of his true nature that he or she is spirit and not the body. This does not make the intellect evil. It is simply that we need to use the intellect as our servant rather than let it become our master through ignorance.

The words good and evil show the duality of the mind always having to choose between what one perceives as right or wrong, thereby being in a continuous state of reaction. The two horns on the mythological figure of the Devil represents this duality.

We must understand and know that there is a difference between thinking a thought and reacting to stimulus external to the self.

External to the self does not necessarily mean external to the body. The 'self', we must remember, is the true self – that of spirit. Note that I do not say 'a spirit'. We are not a spirit. We are spirit manifesting in substance. You cannot separate spirit from spirit or life from life. There are countless expressions of that *one* spirit or life. But it is all *one*.

We could say (when considering the limitations of words) that we are an 'individual point of expression' of that one life or spirit so long as there is no sense of separation attached to that expression. It is the 'oneness' expressing through the countless.

External to the self therefore also means that which abides in the subconscious mind. For example it may be an old memory based on fear or guilt, and as such, when we come into contact with some experience, person or object that reminds us or prompts this old memory, it triggers a reaction. This process applies to both positive and negative memories and most of the time we are unaware of the true cause of our reactions, as it has been buried over many years under denial reactions and we gradually lose sight of the true cause of our problems.

The fear or guilt memory, for example, that has been triggered then attracts an emotional response which adds power or energy to the reaction which in turn stimulates a chemical reaction. This echoes through the nervous system throwing out of harmony the magnetic flow around the body and it can instantaneously, or on a more gradual basis, filter through to the physical body as dis-ease.

Any vibration based on these negative conditions such as guilt or fear is not in tune with the harmonic vibrations of the mind or the physical body.

The reader should keep in mind that these reactions are at times almost constant and it's the continuous repetition of these negative vibrations that eventually manifest as some kind of condition.

It is not hard for the reader to accept and understand

this type of process, even those who do not accept the law of mind over matter should at least see this process in action.

We only need to consider someone who gets such a fright that their hair turns white instantly.

They have not been touched physically yet there has been a physical manifestation of a reaction to a fear that lies in the subconscious.

Dr Mac talks about our state of mind and its affect on our digestive juices in his book, *Heal Yourself*, (page 112), "You know that anger in a mother poisons the milk and the babe becomes cross, irritable and sick; but when the mother's mind is happy, joyful and cheerful, the milk is pure, and the child laughs and is happy."

We have got to realise that the physical is a reflection of the mind and emotions. There is no separation.

It is the subtle causes that we need to turn our attention to. I refer here to our 'attitudes' and our 'motives'.

Our attitude to circumstances or people has a tremendous influence on our mental, emotional and physical health and wellbeing.

Any negative attitude has the effect of constantly undermining our health and short circuiting our nervous system, which finds its expression in our thoughts, words and deeds.

We should look on our thoughts, attitudes and motives as seeds. We should remember that a seed will stay true to its kind. In other words, if we are to plant a mango seed, we cannot hope to harvest tomatoes.

These seeds will bear their fruit. It maybe in our

circumstances, our health or our finances. They will certainly make themselves known to us as age sets in if we have continued to ignore them throughout our life.

A poor attitude towards others can, for example, reflect on the skin, creating some kind of skin condition. It is the skin that is the organ in closest contact to others.

A sour attitude can affect the digestive system and so on. Like attracts like. It is the same with motive. The underlying motives of our actions, words and thoughts will bring a reward in line with its nature.

We must be ever vigilant and do as Paul tells us and 'stand porter at the door of the mind'.

The question is do we have the dedication, courage and honesty to watch our thoughts? This is not a quest for wimps. A man may have the courage to face many physical dangers but cower away at the first suggestion or hint that he should take a critical look at himself.

We tend to keep our focus on things in the world around us, trying to anticipate what will come up next and be in a state of readiness to the best of our ability to meet such a challenge.

Isn't it marvellous how it is always something you least expect. Isn't this in itself proof of an inside job? So we have seen here that our attitudes and our motives need to be right.

My teacher put it this way, "The motive is always greater than the deed. The *why* you do rather than *what* you do."

Dr Mac tells us that, "A change in attitude stimulates the Gangelion mass of nerves. This change for the better frees up the knots that impair the flow of the magnetic energy throughout our being and we greatly benefit from this."

Once such things are bought to our notice (to the notice of those who are genuine in their quest for enlightenment) they can experience 'anxiety', because we suddenly realise that all this time, when we thought that we were doing quite well living a positive and spiritual life, that in reality we are just at the embryo stage of our growth.

This anxiousness is now yet another negative that has to be dealt with.

So we begin to see the process of action/reaction. Just the same as when Jason cut off the head of the dragon others would grow and so it goes on and on and we do not know which way to turn.

There is a way and it is when we start confronting and dealing with these conditions in the subconscious that we truly understand what the Master meant when he said, "Narrow is the way, which leads unto life, and few there be that find it." (Mat 7:14.). We cannot hope to find something that is within if we are too busy looking out in the external world of illusion.

Once we realise that we need to turn inward within ourselves, then the Bible starts to make a whole lot more sense.

Because we know that we are consciousness and intelligence manifesting in matter we can understand and appreciate to a greater degree what is meant when it says "The kingdom of heaven is within you." (Lk:17-21).

The way to start dealing with these usurpers of spirit

is in reality quite simple. It does require dedication, honesty and courage. We have already started our journey by first cleaning up the body. Now we deal with the mind and emotions.

It is no shame that a person finds he or she cannot at first look into the mirror of the self.

Every single Master and those of greatness have had to take on this quest and it is referred to in myths and legends throughout the ages.

The main key to understanding these ancient myths and legends is to realise that the monster they were fighting or circumstances they are confronted with was a part of themselves that they had to deal with. Perhaps hate, envy, jealously, fear, or guilt, etc.

Unless we know *how* to deal with these inner demons (which are only habit patterns functioning in the subconscious mind and not some external demon that some would have you believe) we will simply continue to go around in circles reacting to the same things in life and bringing about the same conditions that tend to make us miserable.

We need to break out of the rut, but we need to know how to do it effectively rather than just again suppressing these forces, which is what usually happens.

To suppress energy is to make it stronger. If a fear was to surface and let's say that it was 100 watts of energy, we then suppress it rather than deal with it and in doing so we use 20 watts of energy to push it back down into the subconscious. The next time it rises up to be dealt with it will now be 120 watts and so on. This is just an example but it serves to show how it works.

The subconscious mind loves habit patterns and it is these inner concepts and thought patterns (positive and negative) having been planted there as we grow up and experience life that create and shape our personality consciousness.

This personality or false self wants to leave things as they are and does not like the habit patterns upset or tampered with. The moment we start to deal with them the subconscious will send up all manner of things to try offset and deter this action.

It must be understood that the subconscious does not know good and evil. While it likes its habit patterns it does not determine that this is good and this is evil. It just produces the results of what is placed in the subconscious mind.

Knowing this then we realise that if we were to get the cooperation of the subconscious mind then there is nothing that we cannot achieve. We need to get it excited and encourage it. Make it enthusiastic as you would a child about anything that are your plans, whatever they may be. This applies to all aspects of our lives and is a 'key' to success.

We are at the point now where we are aware that we are spirit and not the body. That we are birthless and deathless.

We have also pinpointed the centre of all our problems and we realise that these causes are within us and not coming from the external world.

It is of utmost importance to first realise that memories cannot harm us. Things that we may have done, no matter how stupid or selfish and self-centred they may have been, are stumbling blocks only until we turn to face them at which point they then become stepping stones.

The key to dealing with the things of the subconscious mind is the 'science of relaxation'. I say a science for that is just what it is. Dr Mac dedicated a whole book to this subject and if you are fortunate enough to get a copy then you will appreciate the rediscovery of this wonderful science. The book is entitled, *How to Relax and Revitalise Yourself.*

I did mention that the process is simple, but I also said that it would take dedication. In other words, we need to put it into practice. We cannot hope to get results without putting it into action. It only requires 20 minutes a day.

Chapter Thirteen

Putting knowledge into practice

The process is the same as I have explained in the section on leaving the body. However, I will repeat and expand on it here so that the reader wishing to put it into practice does not have to flip backwards and forwards through the book.

After loosening tight clothing, belts ties, etc., lie on a firm bed, place a pillow under your head, supporting the neck, upper shoulders and head. Place another pillow under the knees with the feet about half a metre apart. The arms should be down your side with the hands resting in the groin area. Relax your jaw. Drop the lower jaw then close the lips. Close your eyes.

Relax, breathing normally and talk to your body beginning with the limbs. (If the arms and legs are not relaxed then the rest of the body cannot relax). Talk to your body. It will respond.

"Legs and arms relax, relax, let go, let go."

After 20 minutes while in the relaxed state breathe deeply and repeat, "Divine peace fills me," 60 times. This is done each day as a final exercise before ending your relaxation period.

However, there is a time between when you reach total

relaxation and before this exercise ends that you can enjoy the total weightless and relaxed feeling by placing yourself in the safe hands of nature and floating as if on a cloud. This is a very good practice.

After a few days of learning to first relax the arms and legs, which includes the feet, hands, fingers and toes, you then go to the next area which is the chest muscles.

First relax the limbs as before, then talk to the chest muscles. To get the breathing right, first place the tongue to the roof of the mouth and turn it back into the throat. This allows a much freer action of breathing. Once you have established this breathing the tongue goes back to the floor of your mouth, relax your lower jaw and breathe without effort.

Tell your chest muscles to relax, relax, let go, let go, as before.

Each week when you feel that you have relaxed the progressive sections of the body then add the next area.

After the chest area, include the abdomen area then the back muscles. Do not be too hasty in trying to get through to the end of the list. Remember that the whole idea is relaxation, not impetuousness. How can you relax if you do not patiently and diligently apply the method?

Then add the neck muscles and after that the facial muscles including the eyes and eyelids, the ears and the brow.

As you lie in this state of relaxation you scan every part of your body, telling each and every muscle to relax and let go.

You already know that it is possible and indeed desirable to leave the body and even though you are not actively seeking it during these relaxation exercises, it may come about naturally, and you know not to fear it but to allow yourself the experience of it.

Now that we have been practicing this wonderful science of relaxation and have attained the state of complete relaxation, we can now practice a method Dr Mac calls 'out-cropping by free association'.

You repeat whatever comes into your mind silently to yourself letting one word or event suggest another. You must not inhibit your thought. You will be prepared for this as you have already been told that painful memories and fears cannot hurt you.

You view your mental make up as you would a film. You tell on yourself all the things you did and did not do and should have done.

All these must flow freely before you. In this way you will overcome your own repression. There must be no analysis or judgement of right or wrong, this only hinders the outcropping.

You see now why I said it takes courage and honesty. This is true courage. But you can do it simply by continually following the exercises faithfully.

Do not repress any emotions. Let it all come out. If it is swearing so be it, it will not foul your mouth. Let it go. Many thoughts will rise in regard to sex. These have mostly been repressed in the past, evil thoughts you may have attached to sex. In this way you will acquire a healthy and normal feeling about sex. When you understand the function properly you will know that there is nothing evil about it. This evil was created in your mind.

Any thoughts or feelings you have of fear and anger, let them go. See them as experiences that you have gone through on your road to self-realisation. In this way the energy that is their make up is 'transmuted' from the negative expression to a positive. This energy comes available to you and will reflect in your life as health, wealth and happiness and you will suddenly find that people are attracted to you as your personality gains a positive magnetism.

To the observant reader it now becomes obvious that any thought that we entertain, we attach a good or evil tag to it out of ignorance.

This is emotion which is power, so in effect we are empowering that thought or concept by turning it into a little power plant that is sitting in the subconscious, influencing our mind, emotions, body and circumstances.

The method given is safe and very effective. But it is up to you to put it into practice.

If the Masters were to turn up on planet Earth this is exactly the kind of instructions that they will be suggesting.

You have the chance now instead of having to wait for their guidance to be able to assist them in their service to others.

This service is and has been continual for thousands of years for those who have diligently sought the path.

Yet I tell you that it is the interplay of spiritual forces that apply on the Earth which now allows for much easier access to such things than ever before.

In concluding this section I will share with you a further step that can be put into practice once you have gained total relaxation and feel that it has changed your life.

Once you start putting into practice this exercise of relaxation that has been given to you, it will be something that will thrill you at the very thought of it and you will eagerly look forward to the next session. Relaxation will become a part of your life. Your whole being will reflect a quiet confidence and a reassurance to those about you. It will be to others like a magic healing oil that soothes their wounds in heart and mind. What a wonderful gift.

While in your relaxed state, repeat over and over. "I and the Father are ONE."

Again, do not think about it or apply concepts to it. Just feel it and learn to see the Oneness of all life. Let this realisation dawn in you. There is no rush, no need to become anxious, for now you have found a way.

Resist the urge to run out and tell your friends. Silence is golden, indeed it is power. First, become an example of it yourself and let them come to you. Once they have asked then you know that they are ready and want to know and are therefore receptive to this priceless information.

Chapter Fourteen

A divine discontent

So far we have dealt with preparing ourselves physically, mentally and emotionally in order to be in tune with the new age influences and, most importantly, we have been given the understanding that we are spirit and not the body.

As the influence of the Age of Aquarius continues to take hold, there will be a quickening in the atmosphere and the vibrations of the Earth and all living things including humanity will become finer.

Our Earth and all planets are continually in a state of change. They are manifesting from the etheric state through to the physical state and then returning to the etheric state.

The planets of Mercury, Venus, Mars, Jupiter and Saturn tend to make this journey much at the same rate as our Earth. Whereas the outer planets of Uranus, Neptune and Pluto make this journey at a faster rate, which seems to be timed so that they turn up for the beginning and endings of the ages of the fixed signs of the Zodiac. (Taurus, Leo, Scorpio and Aquarius.)

Thus, their influence unsettles, changes, destroys and regenerates our attitudes, our thinking and social habits in order to bring in the respective new age.

It will be discovered that there are other planets in our solar system, which at this point are in the etheric state and therefore invisible to us for now.

The Earth, having reached its most physical expression during the age of Taurus (Earth element), is now approaching the halfway point on its way back to the most etheric state which will be in the age of Scorpio (water element).

The halfway points of this process, ie., Leo (fire element) and Aquarius (air element) is where the Photon Belt flows through the Zodiac, thus creating what is termed a Golden Age.

This Photon Belt is a band of pure light, and once we entered properly, has the effect that there will be no darkness anywhere, even in the deepest cave.

This is a time of great learning and communication as it allows communication with other planets and solar systems that will be even easier than picking up the phone we use to-day.

For those who are prepared for this transformation there is an automatic upliftment in consciousness as the scales fall from our eyes and we take on our true nature as the Christ self and there is much rejoicing as we consciously reunite with those friends and loved ones we thought had died, and also with those who have been our guides in spirit while we are incarnate.

We also come into contact with great spiritual beings of love and wisdom, the likes of which we cannot even begin to imagine.

While the Earth is in this light state, conditions allow for these great beings to walk the Earth as they have done in times now long forgotten and, having done so, left as reminders great architectural structures that point the way of the true self.

There are higher and higher planes of consciousness and once we reach the Christ self state (the Son) we then begin our expansion into cosmic consciousness (the Father). "No one cometh to the Father except by me." (Jn:14-6).

Access to those on the higher planes of consciousness is available to all right now through taking advantage of the ability of what is termed astral travel. This term is, in reality, not a correct term as we are able and indeed encouraged to visit the higher planes far beyond that of the astral. This takes much dedication and practice, but it is available to all.

Most of us when we leave the body take with us the mental and emotional baggage and therefore we have spasmodic results.

Our guides are always there encouraging us, but most times saddled with our guilt and inferior complexes we fail to take advantage of this gift. Hence, we can now see the value and appreciate the exercises I have given earlier.

That is why I say that it does not matter about what mistakes we may have made in the past. Let them go and turn them into stepping stones NOW by realising your true birthright.

Dr Mac tells us that you cannot do anything tomorrow, nor can you do anything yesterday. It is the NOW that is eternal.

Due to the orbit of our solar system around the great

central sun (the Logos), we spend some 13,000 years out of the Photon Belt during which time the neophyte gradually loses sight of his or her true birthright and treads the path of the prodigal son. The soul becomes enmeshed in the illusion of separation and goes through all the experiences of the sin of separation until once again the realisation dawns in us and we return to the Father in full consciousness of our Christ self.

What happens to those who are not enlightened enough to make the Photon leap? Well, I can assure you all that they are not thrown into some pit of fire and condemned for all eternity.

Just as our planets revolve around our sun at different distances, ie., Mercury is closer than Venus, Venus is closer than Earth and so on, so it is that some solar systems that revolve around the great central sun (Logos) are closer in than ours and therefore spend less time out of the enlightened state (Photon Belt).

Those that are close in to the Logos like our Mercury is to our sun would always be in the light. And therefore always be in that state which we refer to as heaven. All of these solar systems have their own particular states of evolution, far different from what our mortal minds can comprehend.

To try and introduce to the reader the scope on endless creation, I will quote a section from Dr Mac's book, *Life Everlasting*, page 101.

"The universe we know, vast as it appears to be, forms one of a series, and in this series it forms but a small portion of the whole, yet within the whole and not separate from it. Our Sun is a projection of a still more anterior and interior sun which, in turn was projected from a sun anterior to it, and so on till we reach the grand parental Sun around which each and all universes revolve forming a Universe of Universes. I am told that the great central Sun has millions of suns, thousands of times larger than ours, with their planets which form a part of a still greater system, which in turn revolves round a mightier and more central Sun. Our minds whirl with the thoughts of the vastness of it all."

Knowing this now and also realising that other great beings that inhabit these other solar systems are our brothers and sisters and not some type of alien stranger.

We can understand that like attracts like and that each individual is automatically drawn to the solar system (remembering that they are not physical systems as we know it but higher planes on the mental and spiritual levels) that best serves the next stage of our spiritual development.

Some will stay with our present solar system and this is not because they have failed or are some kind of sinner and therefore left behind. Quite the contrary. Some stay so as to gradually become teachers and sages and inspire the next lot of neophytes that arrive at this level of consciousness along the path. It is important to understand that the Father judges no one.

We, through our ignorance, judge ourselves and even worse, we continue to judge ourselves over and over and we remain caught up in the illusion of the 'one sin of the world' – the sense of separation.

While it is necessary to constantly observe our thoughts and our motives and attitudes, it is unnecessary to continue to dwell on a specific deed or failing that we committed because this tends to either cause us to repeat the act over and over or set up a complex in the subconscious mind that only serves to hinder our health and happiness.

When will we enter this Photon Belt proper?

I cannot give you an exact date or even a year. I can tell you that scientists are continuing to monitor an ever increasing presence of light particles in our atmosphere. This being the case then I'd suggest that the year 2012 could prove very interesting.

As we enter this belt in the final stages we will experience a series of phenomena in the sky with the sun not rising and the stars appearing to be continually falling. In reality we have a great deal to look forward to.

Once we get this understanding of how we are an important part of a structured evolutionary process and realise that death is the great lie, we can join Saint Paul when he says in 1 Corinthians 15:55, "O death, where is thy sting? O grave, where is thy victory?" We need to let go of our preconceived ideas. Let go of our concepts, fears, guilt, and all the complexes that assail the mind from their stronghold in the sub-conscious mind.

How is it possible to know ourselves, to know God if we continually place these false gods before him? This is the true meaning of Exodus: 20-3. The gods that the commandment refers to are the concepts and misconceptions and the complexes that I have referred to. We place these false gods (slides) before the light and they reflect in our circumstances, our health, etc. on the screen of life.

Chapter Fifteen

A wheel within a wheel

The question of astrology often comes up with those who are interested in philosophy and biblical matters.

So what's this ancient science all about?

We can approach this question from several different levels of understanding and manifestation.

In reality the Zodiac is the blueprint of evolution.

We can use it to trace the history of ancient civilisations so long as we understand the nature of each sign of the Zodiac.

If we take a look at the Bible for example we can clearly see a written record of the ages from Taurus through to Pisces. During the age of Taurus people worshiped the calf and their weapons were made from copper. This age was when mankind reached the most physical expression after the journey from the etheric state (Scorpio).

The metal of copper is ruled by Venus and it is Venus that is the ruler of Taurus.

We know that a Messiah arrives on the Earth to lead mankind from the old age to the new. Moses led the Children of Israel (although portrayed as the Jews in the story, the word 'Israel' does not represent any specific nation.

It is made up of a combination of the ancient Egyptian gods. For example:

IS. Isis represents the mind or the psyche.

RA. The Sun God. Represents the physical.

EL. (Ellah or Allah) represents the spiritual.

So those who express the spiritual (EL) through mind and body or thought, word and deed, (IS & RA) are the children of ISRAEL.

"God is no respecter of person." (Acts:10-34). So how can God favour a particular race?

Moses stopped worshiping in the old ways and bought in the new ways in line with the incoming new age of Aries. Aries is a fire sign and its symbol is the lamb or ram. The point of the body ruled by Aries is the head and it is ruled by the planet Mars.

Understanding this, we can now see how it all fits together in that, iron (ruled by Mars) replaced copper as weapons. The lamb was sacrificed by fire and the head was anointed with oil.

Then as the age of Aries was to pass away another Messiah came to take mankind from that old age to the new age of Pisces. This, of course, was the Master Jesus.

Pisces is a water sign. It rules the feet and its symbol is the two fishes. Hence, baptism with water became the new way. The fish became the symbol of Christianity and the Master would wash the feet of his 12 disciples. The 12 disciples representing the 12 signs of the Zodiac.

The opposite sign to each of these is very important, as you need the positive and negative effect in all things.

The opposite sign of Taurus is Scorpio and Scorpio represents secrets and secret places. Therefore, together with the influence of an earthy age (Taurus) we see many secret temples constructed at this time.

The opposite sign of Aries is Libra. This represents the scales of justice and we saw how Moses came down from Mount Sinai with the two tablets of the Ten Commandments – the law as laid down by God.

The opposite sign of Pisces is Virgo. The true symbol that represents Virgo is a young girl holding five ears of grain.

Well, we know that the Master Jesus was said to be born of the Virgin (Virgo). We also know that the Master fed the multitude the five loaves of bread (represented by the ears of grain) and the two fishes, which is the symbol of Pisces. All of these events and symbols have much deeper esoteric meanings.

The Ten Commandments, although they apply to the physical life, also have a much higher meaning which the aspiring neophyte learns and becomes responsible for once he or she gets to a certain level of understanding. This applies to all the stories in the Bible and in all sacred writings.

There is the meaning that assists and guides us in our social structure, but there is also that inner deeper meaning that serves to show the way of the path of enlightenment back to self-realisation.

Unfortunately, even a great number of the interpretations of the lesser meanings are incorrect because they are based on the belief of a God external to the self due to the 'sense of separation'.

I have already given the reader one example of the story of the prodigal son. I explained that when we get caught up in the illusions of the external world we take on the journey of the prodigal son until finally the realisation of our At-One-Ment with the Father dawns within us.As an example of these higher meanings, I will quote the author, Corinne Heline, from her book entitled, *The Bible and the Stars*:

"The parables also have their astrological interpretation. The parable of the Prodigal Son is the journey of the sun through the 12 signs. The older son represents the objective activity and the plenteous bounty which the sun brings forth when above the horizon; the younger son, the 'mighty famine in the land', or the cold and darkness of winter, when the sun travels below the horizon.

Ancient astrologers referred to the horizon as the Place of Birth (Spring Equinox) and the Place of Death (Autumn Equinox). Horus, the Egyptian Sun God, was known as the God of two horizons.

As the Resurrection Season, the son or sun returns to the Father's house, this is the time of rejoicing throughout all nature, the time of a 'cosmic sunrise'. The son (sun) that was dead is alive again. The banquet of nature's bounties is spread for the glad Easter of the Resurrection Season. (Northern Hemisphere.)"

Once we start to see and understand that the stories and parables are referring to seasonal events and celestial planetary movements then the ancient writings start to reveal themselves to us.

To go up a mountain or a high place actually means a higher state of consciousness, to leave the physical plane of consciousness and return to our true home.

I mentioned that particular story because it clearly shows the link of the resurrection at Easter as it is celebrated with the Spring Equinox events in nature that Corinne refers to. This shows how every thing is linked. That in nature itself there is a rejoicing with the coming back of the sun. This, like all the seasonal events is a very special time for prayer, meditation and contemplation. This is what it really means to be one with nature. To understand, respect and take advantage of these special times for our spiritual growth. This cannot be done if we feel or believe that we are separate from life.

Corinne explains in *The Bible and the Stars* that Jacob had four wives. Leah, her handmaid Zilpah, Rachel and her handmaid, Billah. While Jacob represents the sun, each of his four wives represented the four phases of the moon. For example, Leah represents the full moon. Zilpah, the last quarter, Rachel, the new moon and Billah, the first quarter.

Between them they had 12 children which of course represents the 12 signs of the Zodiac. (Actually, they had 13 children when you count Dinah, which is necessary as she represents Virgo. The number of children comes back to 12 when you count two as one, ie., Simeon and Levi who represent the sign of Gemini, the twins).

Once we know which of the wives (moon phases) gave birth to which child and in turn understand which child represents which Zodiac sign, this then gives us a time of each calendar month which is conducive to prayer and meditation.

This tells us that it is not necessarily the full moon that is the highlight of every month. Although Leah (full moon) did produce seven of the 13 children including Simeon and Levi, which effectively brings her number back to six.

In addition to this information the four moon phases also represent, on a monthly basis, the two solstices and the two equinoxes, ie., Leah as the full moon represents the Summer Solstice. Billah, as first quarter, represents the Spring Equinox. Rachel, as the new moon, represents the Winter Solstice, and Zilpah, as last quarter, represents the Autumn Equinox.

These times, once we understand them, can be taken advantage of by the neophyte on the long journey home.

We can also include the music of the spheres, which was written by our musical geniuses. Corinne explains in her book, *Colour and Music in the New Age*, that music was written to harmonise and invoke the natural forces of the solstices and equinoxes.

I can vouch for the effect of playing the right music to suit the respective solstices and equinoxes. Years ago I grew Sim carnations in two large nurseries on a commercial scale. Every solstice and equinox I would play the music at the right moment. I would work out the exact time of the solstice or equinox and I would time the music I was to play for that time. For example, 'Midsummer Night's Dream' would have about four records for the whole piece and if it took two hours and 20 minutes and the Summer Solstice was due at 2.10 a.m., then I would count back one hour and 10 minutes, which in this case would be 1 a.m. So I would start the music at 1 a.m. so that it reached its crescendo at 2.10 a.m.

The result was that even in these high-bred carnations

I had perfume where previously there was none. The flowers were large and bursting with colour.

The music for these seasons are as follows:

Spring Equinox: Handel's Messiah and Wagner's Parsifal.

Summer Solstice: Mendelssohn's Midsummer Night's Dream and Wagner's Die Meistersinger.

Autumn Equinox: Bach's Passion Of Saint Matthew and Wagner's Tannhauser.

Winter Solstice: Schubert's Ave Maria and Wagner's Lohengrin.

The information that lists the moon phases and the signs of the Zodiac is in the following table:

MOTHER	MOON PHASE	CHILD	ZODIAC SIGN	ELEMENT
LEAH	FULL	REUBEN	AQUARIUS	AIR
LEAH	FULL	SIMEON	GEMINI	AIR
LEAH	FULL	LEVI	GEMINI	AIR
LEAH	FULL	JUDAH	LEO	FIRE
LEAH	FULL	ISAACHAR	TAURUS	EARTH
LEAH	FULL	ZEBULUM	PISCES	WATER
LEAH	FULL	DINAH	VIRGO	EARTH
ZILPAH	LAST QUARTER	GAD	ARIES	FIRE
//	//	ASHER	LIBRA	AIR
RACHEL	NEW	JOSEPH	SAGITARIUS	FIRE
//	//	BENJAMIN	CANCER	WATER
BILLAH	FIRST QUARTER	DAN	SCORPIO	WATER
//	//	NAPHALI	CAPRICORN	EARTH

It can be argued that the full moon is the most important time of the monthly cycle due to the axis of each of the signs.

I have mentioned that the opposite sign of any given sign is very important in the functions of astrology. Those astrologers who study astrodiagnosis realise that any given disease or condition may well manifest in the part of the body ruled by the sign that is opposite to the sign in difficulty. For this reason the full moon phase which has the sun in a given sign and the moon opposite (full moon) would be covering this axis very well.

If we check our Table we can see that four of the six signs have their opposite sign under the full moon influence (Leah). For example, Aquarius and its opposite sign Leo, and Pisces and its opposite sign Virgo.

That leaves Taurus, which has its opposite sign Scorpio under the influence of first quarter (Billah). Gemini has its opposite sign of Sagittarius under the influence of the new moon (Rachel).

This points to a deeper meaning and influence of these moon phases in their respective signs and not to take for granted that the full moon is the most powerful time of the month.

The sign of Aries, which is the time of the year of the Spring Equinox (Northern Hemisphere), is born of the last quarter moon phase. Libra, which is the time of the year of the Autumn Equinox, is also under the last quarter moon phase. Cancer, which is the time of the Northern Hemisphere Summer Solstice, is under the sign of the new moon. Capricorn, which is the Winter Solstice is under the first quarter moon phase.

SIGN	ELEMENT	MONTH	MOON PHASE	MEDITATION
ARIES	FIRE	MARCH 21 APRIL 20	LAST QUARTER	A recharging of Self which ignites enthusiasm, confidence and hope.
TAURUS	EARTH	APRIL 20 MAY 21	FULL MOON	Manifesting the outpouring of spiritual harmony.
GEMINI	AIR	MAY 21 JUNE 21	FULL MOON	Breathing exercises to harmonise and observe our thoughts.
CANCER	WATER	JUNE 22 JULY 23	NEW MOON	Feeling and being at one with the soul of nature.
LEO	FIRE	JULY 23 AUG23	FULL MOON	The heart is the doorway , the eye and the ear of the spirit.
VIRGO	EARTH	AUG 23 SEPT 23	FULL MOON	Reflect your inner peace and wisdom to all humanity.
LIBRA	AIR	SEPT 23 OCT 24	LAST QUARTER	Still the mind and know that still small voice.
SCORPIO	WATER	OCT 24 NOV 22	FIRST QUARTER	Observe your motives, desires and attitudes.
SAGGITARIUS	FIRE	NOV 22 DEC 22	NEW MOON	The still flame of a candle inspires intuition.
CAPRICORN	EARTH	DEC 22 JAN 21	FIRST QUARTER	Letting go of the concepts. Pruning the tree.
AQUARIUS	AIR	JAN 21 FEB 19	FULL MOON	Enter the six-pointed star to find the Christ Self within.
PISCES	WATER	FEB 19 MARCH 21	FULL MOON	Be still and at peace to know life's journey.

So we see that the neophyte and the alchemist can utilise these times of the month for prayer and meditation and it is in the understanding of the four moon phases of the month, which are microscopic representations of the solstices and equinoxes that he or she can get the most from the forces that are at play on the Earth at that time.

In addition, we take into consideration the element of the sign so that we can be more in tune with the celestial and terrestrial forces.

The table on the preceding page can assist with meditation suggestions. The information is simply to allow you to arrange your times of meditation and prayer while utilising the best times of the days, weeks and months.

A very good series of meditation suggestions and further information is available in the book by Joan Hodgson entitled *Planetary Harmonies, An Astrological Book on Meditation.*

While such studies can be informative, of great value and of great interest, the reader should be careful not to get caught up in their ritual and rhetoric because if they are used in that way one tends to lose sight of the goal which is self-realisation.

Far too often an aspiring soul falls prey to the false ego that likes to impress those about them through colourful and mystical ceremony.

This message is given by the Master Jesus in Saint Matthew 6:5,6. To go into the closet and close the door is referring to meditation and being rewarded openly is the manifestation of your union with the Father within.

Jesus goes on to talk about what he terms vain repetitions (affirmations). The key to understanding this is to know the true meaning of what is meant by: "As a man thinketh *in his heart*, so is he." (Prov: 23.7) It is the deepest thought that will manifest. For example, repeating an affirmation about health. You have in your mind both the desire for good health and the not having good health. This is typical of the duality of the mind.

The thought that will manifest is the one that is strongest or deepest, such as the 'wanting' on the one hand and the 'not having' on the other.

Usually and unfortunately, the not having is the strongest because we do not know the law and not knowing the law we lack that vital ingredient called faith.

We have the subconscious notion that we are not worthy, that we are full of sin and must grovel to some external mighty being for forgiveness.

These are the slides in the projector. Put them aside and forget them. You no longer have need of them. We are all sons of God gradually unfolding to the realisation of that fact. We don't have to earn it. We are that NOW.

The wording of an affirmation is also extremely important and although this situation has been addressed to some degree these days I think that due to the importance of this subject it is worth further comment.

I have mentioned that the subconscious mind is like a child. Knowing this then we should be very wary about what information we feed into it because we now know that it will give back results in the exact nature of what is given to it.

If we were to repeat over and over something like "Day by day my asthma is getting better and better." We are in effect focusing the subconscious mind's attention on the condition of asthma, literally assuring it an existence.

By saying, "my asthma or my..." (whatever condition or circumstance), we are owning it. We are welding it into the subconscious mind and actually bring about the law of reverse effect.

Dr Mac, through many years of experience of healing and teaching, has put together the following, which does not hinder the results, rather it encourages the manifestation of total good health. This is best repeated while in the relaxed state as already explained. "Day by day in every way, I am getting better and better."

The reader will notice that this approach does not concentrate on a given condition and also, most importantly, it does not limit itself in any way.

Imagine someone who desires wealth and creates an affirmation that's worded, "I am going to win tomorrow's one million dollar lotto."

Firstly, we have the duality in the subconscious mind of the wanting and the not having. Then we have a reference of a time that will never come about. For example, 'tomorrow'. (The only time that exists is NOW.) Secondly, we have limited the amount by stating an amount of one million dollars.

If you say, "What's wrong with the amount of one million dollars?" then you have missed the point it could be one billion but it is the 'limitation' that is placed on the subconscious mind that serves to not bring about your desires.

The subconscious mind is not impressed by one million dollars as we may be. A limit in any form is a violation of universal law because it only knows 'infinite'. The subconscious mind is limitless. So be careful that you do not restrict it from doing its work for you.

We need to remember that all of nature and all associated with the creation and evolution of man are anxious to help us. It is ourselves that hinder their assistance with the stupid beliefs and concepts of not being worthy or some such rubbish.

Do we really think that by believing and feeling this way that we are being humble? I have always liked the saying, "Let go and let God." We need to die to the old intellectual personality and take on the garment of Christ (our true self).

Paul put it this way, "Let this mind be in you the mind of Christ." (Phil. 2-5).

The 'letting go' is an art in itself. It is something that you cannot make yourself do, just as you cannot make yourself go to sleep. It is a surrendering to the state of just being and the better we are at achieving that process the more there is God and the less there is of you (the personality).

Chapter Sixteen

Way of the healer

Many times we have said to ourselves and to others, What can I do?" when confronted with the suffering of people, including children in countries ravaged with draught and wars. There is this feeling of being totally inadequate as we try to come up with some magic idea that will be the answer to these seemingly insurmountable situations.

How often have we heard someone say, "How can God let this happen?" It is not God that brings these situations about, but rather the ignorance of Man. It is the ignorance of our true birthright that brings about the sense of separation. This in turn leads to greed, hate, racism and violence.

How would it be possible for anyone who is totally aware of the 'Oneness' of all life to inflict such atrocities on another? Because at the same time you would also know that you are actually doing it to yourself. Yet those who wish to avail themselves to the service of healing can achieve a great deal.

In this service one does not have to have university degrees, although no doubt there are some who would tell you this.

There are many misconceptions about the art of

healing and it is my intention, after many years of contact with those who are the healing ministers beyond the flesh, to give information that is in line with universal laws. This will assist anyone to become, not the healer, for we of ourselves can do nothing, but instruments through which the healing ministers of Christ may operate through.

Here, we come to know yet another important reason why we should keep our bodies in good health and especially drink a great deal of water and health fluids. Water is a conductor. We all know this, so it is natural that if we wish to assist the ministers in healing, then we should make sure that there is plenty of fluid taken into our body so that we are able to conduct the power that comes through us. How can we do this if we are like a dried up prune?

There are several methods of spiritual healing that a small group of people can become active in. There is the laying on of hands, absent healing and healing through prayer.

It is written, "Where two or three are gathered in my name, there am I also." (Mt:18-20). So when people gather together in the name of the living Christ in simplicity, dedication and sincerity, we are assured that there are those who are the healing ministers of Christ that will be attracted to your humble meeting because the Master has told us so.

Again here do not get caught up in some grandiose, elaborate ceremony. It is totally unnecessary and may I say detrimental to the power of healing and prayer. For how can one be dedicated to the healing of others if one is too busy with ceremony and rituals.

Intense concentration and mantras are also not necessary. It is simply the coming together of those who are sincere of heart and allow themselves to be instruments of those beyond the flesh who serve Christ.

You can have a candle; you can have a picture of the Master as you conceive him to be, or flowers and gentle music to set the mood and relax you. You can have a cross. But keep it simple and do not place too much importance on such things.

Have a room or an area in your home that is especially suited for your meetings. That is not to say that you cannot use the room for other things but when it comes to your healing time, be it one night a week or each night, then that area is used for your meeting. This allows for the power to build up, and that is important.

I already referred to 'the etheric body'. The practicing healer should know that it is the etheric body or what we refer to as the etheric 'substance' that is used in healing by the healing ministers.

The etheric body dissipates in death along with the physical body. Therefore those beyond the flesh do not have this body. That is why those of us in flesh are needed for the application of healing.

The etheric body is the connection between spirit and matter and the healing ministers use this etheric substance to 'connect' with those who are ill in order to bring about the healing. The quality of the etheric body is the result of our way of life. The more we strive to be a living example of the Christ Principles the greater the quality of our etheric body.

They take this substance from the etheric body of the healer and use it in their healing work. One can now see why it is so important that many people practice healing if we really want to make an impact on worldwide suffering.

At times when this vital substance is taken from the healer. They may feel a slight depletion in energy. This can be easily remedied through deep natural breathing, and you will find that it is always the case that a little more is added than what was taken. So the healer will, through sincere dedication, gradually build up a magnetic aura and be able to be of further assistance to those about them.

It is a good practice to invite the healing ministers to take from you at any time as they need it.

The importance I referred to before of having the meeting at the same place or point in the house is because you build up an aura of power and this is used by the healing ministers in two ways.

1. They can use the etheric substance of that area once it has built up enough at anytime, the same as they do when they come to you at any time provided you have invited them to do so.
2. It becomes a place where they can bring newly departed souls at any time who have been through some trauma in meeting their death and it makes it much easier to communicate with them so as to explain what has taken place. It is because of the familiar 'more earthy' vibrations of your sanctuary that they feel more at ease and therefore can be reached.

I might explain here that on the other side there is no

time as we know it, and there is no pain because we do not have the physical vehicle. Therefore, when someone is in, shall we say a hysterical state, we cannot slap their face to bring them out of it so to speak. So having such places to bring these souls to is of great assistance. Once they are settled enough they are taken to the healing temples in the great beyond and indeed these temples are something to behold.

Another thing that should be known is that the individual entity that the healing is sent to may reject it. I said entity instead of person because I was referring to the higher self rather than the personality self of the individual who is sent the healing.

As I have mentioned before, we are here to experience life and work out the karma that we have taken on ourselves for this particular lifetime.

It can sometimes apply that the healing will be rejected because the entity needs to go through that particular experience or suffering. That does not mean that they will not at least show some improvement where karma permits; usually to help comfort the loved ones who are concerned for them.

The healing that you sent is not lost or in vain. Rest assured that the healing given goes to someone in need; most likely someone you do not know and will never meet. But it is used and very much appreciated.

Many times over the years we have been told. "You do not know what you do." Meaning, you can never know how much your tiny service of even half an hour per week can do.

We need to be careful about the motive. I cannot stress

this too much. Always keep your motives high and based on selflessness and you can do no wrong.

Be ever mindful of the subtleness of the false ego. It is a very good practice to sit quietly every now and then for the purpose of viewing your motives. You wish to be a healer? Good. Why?

If it is that you feel that your motives are not all they could be. Simply, relax and let it go through your mind how you are. Do not attach any feelings of guilt to it. Just observe. Then let it go through your mind how you would like to be adding to it the emotion or enthusiasm of your desire to be a better example of the Christ self. Then just go about your daily activities, comfortable in the knowledge that all will come to fruition.

I have asked, therefore I shall receive.

For those of you who do not do healing because you think that you are in some way not good enough, let me assure you that even the urge to be of service is proof of a light that shines within you. You can through dedication and sincerity and turn that small glow into the noonday sun.

Your prayer may go like this:

"Lord, take me, even me. For I am not the person that I used to be. I seek to transmute the personality consciousness that I was and take on the Christ consciousness that I really am and become a servant of my fellow man thus being at one with the Father."

Even half an hour per week is an effective amount of time for the practice of healing. An hour is even better but there is no need to draw it out.

If you have people visiting each week then it is best

that the meeting not be drawn out because they will tend to drop away.

Half an hour before people are due to arrive, light your candle, put on your music and set up your table with your picture, etc. if you wish. Let the atmosphere start to build up. When they arrive, there is no need for solemn faces. Friendly greetings and laughter and general chit chat is the way to go. When you go to the healing room, leave the solemn faces outside and take in the cheery, friendliness and enthusiasm that is your natural nature. Just relax, listen to the music while inwardly welcoming and inviting the healing ministers into your centre.

It is best to have a healing list of all those people who you wish to direct healing to. Each week some may be taken off due to their recovery and others may be added because you have come into contact with someone or heard of someone who needs the healing.

Each person at the meeting may pray for someone or one may do all the praying. It is best to pray for the Earth and mankind as a whole first up and then move on to individuals.

In absent healing the person who knows the sufferer sits in the chair as the sufferer and the one who wants to do the healing prayer stands behind the chair with their hands on the shoulders of the seated person while the prayer is said.

In the event that any of those who are attending the meeting need healing there is nothing wrong in saying so and sitting in the chair and letting the others give you a 'charge' as we would say.

The laying on of hands can involve the healer placing

the right hand on the solar plexus area and the left hand on the area of the body that that needs the healing.

This creates a circuit of positive and negative and it is the solar plexus that is the power area.

Read through your list each night, pausing briefly after each name is read.

The Lord's Prayer should be said during the meeting (usually in opening the meeting) as it also is very powerful in healing and raising of consciousness.

Note that it starts with 'Our' Father.

There is a certain way to say this prayer which I will not go into here. The secret is to understand the words of the Lord's Prayer and emphasise and recognise the meaning of these words in their place.

At the end of the meeting after someone has given the closing prayer, thank the healing ministers and re-dedicate yourselves in the work. Just sit quietly listening to the music and bathing in the atmosphere. After a few minutes you can return to general conversation and perhaps share your night's experiences with each other. Do not enter into gossip sessions, etc. This atmosphere is too good for that type of thing. You have taken the time to build up the atmosphere, so lets not deplete it through such things.

Before you leave the sanctuary it is a good idea to seal yourselves. This has nothing to do with superstition or the like; by giving out healing through prayer you have opened your centres and it is best to seal them before re-entering the outside world because it can attract some lower astral influences. This is not something to be fearful of like some evil demon. It is simply a precaution.

I mentioned earlier in the book about the build up of thoughtforms and attitudes that affect the Earth, you will have understanding along the lines that I am referring to.

The way to seal your centres is to mentally place a cross within a circle over the forehead, the heart and the solar plexus and run a silver thread around your entire body six times. This only takes a moment and is a good practice.

In completing this section I need to point out the following in regard to karma. There are those in the past who have asked me if they should see a doctor about a certain condition or have an operation for a particular ailment. They say that if it is their karma then the medical treatment or surgery will not work anyway.

I believe that there is a lot of unnecessary surgery that goes on and over-prescribing of medication, which is now being recognised by the medical profession itself. I would point out to these people, who obviously have very little understanding of the law of karma, that it is also part of their karma to be born into an age of enlightenment where protection, facilities and treatment can be given to them. However, natural treatment in line with nature and in dealing with the causes through the relaxation exercises that I have given will certainly see good results. There must be a willingness to let go of the old concepts. It would be best if we all lived by the old adage that prevention is better than cure.

If we put the exercises into practice as a way of life then we can look forward to a full life of health, wealth and happiness and share in the universal abundance that is omnipresent in nature.

Chapter Seventeen

New start regime

Rules of Eating

1. If not entirely comfortable in mind and body from the previous mealtime, you should miss the next meal.
2. Do not eat unless you have a keen desire for the plainest food.
3. Do not eat beyond your needs.
4. Be sure to masticate your food thoroughly.
5. Miss meals if you are in pain, or if you are emotionally upset or not hungry; chilled or overheated; or during acute illness.
6. Never eat starch and protein together.
7. Have raw vegetables (salads) and starches, sandwiches for midday meal.

Upon Rising

Internal stomach bath

Juice of one lemon in a glass of warm water followed by two glasses of warm water (blood heat). Then lie on your back with a pillow under your buttocks. Distend and relax the walls of the stomach quickly for about one minute.

At first it may seem disagreeable, but after a few mornings it will be taken with relish, as it acts as a stimulant and appetiser and gives you back that inner spark and zest.

Skin Brushing

Use a stiff brush over your entire body in a circular motion. You will tend to use it gently at first but soon get used to it and brush with vigour. This is to be done dry. This will rid the body of dead skin and bring the blood to the surface to enrich the skin. If you faithfully carry out this exercise for one year, you will have skin that will be the envy of others.

After becoming accustomed to your brush you will do well to buy a fresh brush. Scrubbing brushes are recommended.

Go for an early morning walk or do some gardening. Then have a ripe banana mashed to a cream sprinkled with cinnamon. If these suggestions are followed faithfully you will experience a pleasant change in your health and circumstances.

For those who are ill or those who need a complete clean out of the physical body, Dr Mac recommends the following:

Eleven-day elimination regime

A hot Epsom salt bath should be taken every night during this regime; 2 pkts of salts per bath should be enough. Enemas should be used for the first four or five days and then discontinued. Natural movements should then be the aim.

Note: You may choose to have a colonic irrigation which would only be necessary once during the 11- day regime. For enemas get 2 lt of warm water (blood heat), apply one heaped teaspoon of bicarbonate soda and a cap full of glycerine.

Nothing but water and fruit juices, preferably grapefruit, should be taken into the body for the first three days. Drink one glass of juice every four hours of those days. For the next two days have fruit only, such as grapes, melons, tomatoes, pears, peaches and plums. Dried fruits (not sulphur dried) such as prunes, figs, peaches, soaked overnight, and baked apple.

During the following six days breakfast should consist of citrus fruits; have any other kind of fruit between breakfast and lunch. For lunch have a salad of three to six vegetables and two cups of potassium broth.

Potassium broth is made from five diced carrots, a stalk of celery, a handful of parsley and spinach, one onion and tomato and one litre of water; season with whole salt. Simmer for 35 minutes only. If cooked longer the elements deteriorate. Potassium prevents constipation and growths. It is a strong alkaline flushing agency and eliminator and a powerful neutraliser, being cool and antiseptic.

If hungry between meals, you may take fruit or fruit juices.

The evening meal should consist of two or three steamed vegetables and two cups of potassium broth. Fruit juices can be taken before retiring if wanted.

Rigid adherence to the diet is an absolute necessity for anyone endeavouring to regain good health. Eat plenty, though not to satiety.

Once you have completed the 11-day elimination

regime, your body will be free of waste and toxins. So what now? Be very careful that you do not slide back into bad habits.

The following is recommended.

Before breakfast: As already mentioned. Note: never take a shower immediately upon rising.

Breakfast: Two fruits and one protein. The time of the year will decide what fruits are in season. Don't forget dried fruits (soaked overnight) or baked apple.

Suggestions: Sliced figs and cream, half a rockmelon with strawberries. Fruit with cottage cheese and honey. Eat an egg with fruit for variety.

Lunch: Raw salad, one starch and health drink. Rye crisp, or corn bread.

Starches: Potatoes, baked banana (or ripe raw bananas; they should not be eaten unless they are dead ripe). Steamed brown rice, steel cut oatmeal, weetbix, bread (whole wheat, rye or soya). Cereals (oatmeal, shredded wheat, etc.) Sandwiches (not with meat).

Drinks: Vegetable broth, buttermilk, milk or any health drink.

3 o'clock: Fruit of any kind, such as dates, apples, figs, peaches, fruit juices or vegetable juices.

Evening meal: A small raw salad, two cooked vegetables, one protein and a broth or health drink if desired.

Protein: Fish twice a week. Use white fish with fins and scales. Meat, young beef or lamb for first month, twice a week. Never use pork. Cottage cheese twice a week, and omelette once a week.

For complete vegetarian use soya beans, lima beans

and cottage cheese, etc. for your protein intake.

Eat well, eat plenty but not to satiety. Remember to drink plenty of pure water, always. Water is the great cleanser.

Chapter Eighteen

Breathing for health

The following four simple breathing exercises will cleanse the body, cleanse the blood, stimulate the nervous system and expand the chest.

Faithfully carry out these exercises, doing each one six times each in the early morning, and carrying them out before retiring. I can say from experience that they will not only assist greatly in maintaining your health but also assist in bringing about positive circumstances and plans in your daily life. (Dr Mac, *Heal Yourself* p. 50-52.)

How to cleanse the body

Stand erect, inhale a complete natural breath. Now hold the breath, clench your fist, contract the muscles of your arms and legs, then let go and exhale slowly.

This has the effect of sending the blood from the extremities of the legs and arms to the chest cavity. The exhaling will get rid of a great deal of waste matter.

After doing this two or three times you will find a cool, sweet feeling all over your body. This is the result of cleansing the system, and it is done by a simple method of driving the blood from the extremities into the chest cavities. Immediately you contract your muscles you drive the blood into the chest cavities and by doing so the blood is oxygenated.

To cleanse the blood

Take a deep natural breath, at the same time raising up your arms to a horizontal position; then drop your arms by your side loosely; hold your breath as long as you possibly can and then exhale vigorously through the open mouth.

The blood is cleansed by holding the air in the lungs for a considerable time. This gives an opportunity for the blood to be fully oxygenated and give up its waste matter. The vigorous expulsion of the air through the mouth has the effect of cleansing the lungs.

It is an excellent breath for cleansing the blood. You will find your skin become moist, with the result that it tends to clear up skin troubles of long standing. You must hold the breath for some considerable time. When you raise your arms fill your lungs to capacity; then hold and expel vigorously. Practice makes perfect.

How to expand the chest

Stand erect, take a deep natural breath, retain the air, raise your arms in front of you, fists clenched; then throw your arms backwards and sideways as far as possible. Do this several times but do not overdo the exercise. You will find by doing this that your chest will expand a centimetre or two in a very short time. Retain the air while doing the exercise.

When you take a deep breath, swing the arms forwards and backwards as long as you can keep the breath. This expands the chest.

How to stimulate the nervous system

Stand erect, inhale a deep natural breath, retain air, and with your arms by your side perfectly relaxed, gradually contract the fingers until your fists are clenched. Then contract the muscles of your arms, followed by your shoulders, down your chest to your back muscles, down your legs to your feet, then gradually relax your fingers, arms, chest, back, legs and exhale. You will find your nervous system will be vitalised. This exercise stimulates the nervous system and your nerves become as steel.

Handy hints

Lung tonic: Onions or any of the onion family have a powerful effect on the lungs. Drink onion water, garlic or leek water or broth from any of the cooked onion family. Drink at time of coughing, soreness or tenderness in lungs. You may add eucalyptus, honey and drink it hot. Australian honey taken from the blue gum is excellent.

Cough syrup: For extreme coughing pour honey over some cut up onion and let stand all night. Drink one tablespoonful of this juice every hour.

World's best tonic: Egg yolk and orange juice.

For that yellow complexion: Drink plenty of grapefruit juice.

Jaundiced skin: One glass of tomato and sauerkraut

juice every day for a week. Skip a week and then return to this drink again.

Pimples and acne: The secret is keeping the digestive system clean. Refer to section on internal stomach bath.

Perfect skin: Refer to section on skin brushing.

Tighten facial skin and tone up facial muscles: Epsom salt packs, which are made from one teaspoon of Epsom salt to ½ lt of water. Apply hot wet towels and leave on until they begin to get cool. Pinch the face slightly afterwards. Follow this with a skin food made up of ¼ teaspoon of powered garlic to one tablespoon of lanolin. Neck wrinkles can be overcome through neck exercises and Epsom salt packs.

Best antiseptics: Garlic, lemons and onions.

Best foods for kidneys: Asparagus and cauliflower. (Drink plenty of water for good kidney and general health).

Nerve sedative: Onions, lettuce and celery.

Nerve tonic: Carrots, turnips and radishes.

Best food for liver: Tomatoes.

Headaches: Plenty of cool water.

Blood tonic: Carrots and cherries.

Best source of iron: Raw beetroot, apples, raw cabbage, cherries, lettuce and raisins.

Asthma: Its first cause is incorrect breathing. Refer to section on Breathing.

Asthma management: Do not eat starch foods after 3 p.m. Do not over-eat before going to bed. Breathing exercises as given morning and evening, including breathing exercises that strengthen the nervous system.

(Note: Starch food needs exercise in order to digest.

If eaten too close to bedtime they will ferment and the fumes from this can travel up to the oesophagus area which in turn sets off a reaction, triggering a partial closure in the trachea area and an asthma attack is brought on.)

Raw foods are better than cooked. Remember what I mentioned on how to eat our foods.

Quality foods, not quantity

I have found that one can have access to all the knowledge in the world but unless we put it into practice then it is of little use.

The incoming age will challenge all our ideas, and beliefs and in doing so will bring with it a sense of insecurity which, although already in evidence, is only the beginning.

For those who are sincere in their quest for truth and have the conviction and the self-discipline to put into practice the principles of Christ in thought, word and deed will find the inner security that will be priceless at this critical time.

May divine peace come, touch, enter
and remain with you all.

Bibliography

The Holy Bible, (King James Version.)
The Bible and the Stars, Corinne Heline.
Colour and Music in the New Age, Corrine Heline.
Planetary Harmonies, Joan Hodgson. Available at the White Eagle Group, Maleny, Qld.

Books by Dr Murdo McDonald-Bayne:

Heal Yourself.
Life Everlasting. How to Relax and Revitalise Yourself.
I Am the Life.
Beyond the Himalayas.

Authors Note

Even though Dr Mac's books are now out of print. Some works are still being reproduced along with a great list of audio tapes taken from his original talks, available from:
Ms Lora Mendel,
106-840 Kiwanis Way, RR #1,
Gibsons, BC VON 1VO,
Canada.